The Law
and
Your Dog

The Law
and
Your Dog

Edward H. Greene

South Brunswick and New York:
A. S. Barnes and Company
London: Thomas Yoseloff Ltd

A. S. Barnes and Co., Inc.
Cranbury, New Jersey 08512

Thomas Yoseloff Ltd
108 New Bond St.
London W. 1, England

SBN: 498-06769-6

Printed in the United States of America

Preface

I bred my first litter of pups when I was sixteen years of age, and since that time I have enjoyed owning dogs and participating in the activities of dog clubs, as well as sponsoring field trials, kennel clubs, and dog shows. I am always amazed by the lack of knowledge that most people have about the laws governing dogs. This, of course, is due to the lack of uniformity in statutory laws and the absence of a consulting book on dog laws.

Today the dog business is big business; millions of dollars are spent each year in breeding, selling, buying, showing and training dogs. And these activities are going on without the parties involved having a source of reference to guide them as to their rights and liabilities.

I have attempted to set forth the material facts as well as quotations from the Courts' Opinions, so that the reader will obtain a general understanding of the fundamental principles of laws governing dogs. However, this book is not intended to be a substitute for legal advice from an experienced lawyer. If the reader finds himself involved in a transaction or controversy concerning his dog he should ask himself these questions:

"What are my rights?"

"What are my legal responsibilities?"

The primary purpose for writing *The Law and Your Dog* is to enable a person to recognize and appraise his problem and to act in a proper manner to protect his rights.

No useful reference is complete without forms covering the usual agreements needed to properly record transactions involving dogs. Therefore, I have included certain legal forms that I have found to be useful in the various phases of dog business.

I dedicate this book to "Lindy," "Vixen," "Chuck," "Blue Crystal," and "Nannie," and all the other dogs who consider me their friend.

I could not conclude without expressing deep appreciation to the late Thomas G. Lenfestey, not only a gentleman, but one of the outstanding Professional Dog Handlers, who so expertly conditioned, advised and showed our Kerry Blue Terriers. Also, to the late Mrs. Eileen McEachren, owner of Tailteann Kennels, a delightful lady who helped, advised and guided us in starting our Kerry Blue Terrier Kennel. These memories and friendships will always be cherished by my wife and me.

EDWARD H. GREENE

Contents

Contents

A Tribute to the Dog

A speech to the jury by the late Senator Vest of Missouri, in the trial of an action to recover damages for the wanton killing of a dog belonging to a neighbor. Mr. Vest represented the plaintiff who demanded $200 damages. As a result of this speech, the jury after two minutes' deliberation found for the plaintiff and assessed the damages at $500, after asking the Court if the man who had shot the dog could not be punished by imprisonment or be more severely dealt with.

"Gentlemen of the Jury: The best friend a man has in this world may turn against him and become his enemy. His son or daughter that he has reared with loving care may prove ungrateful. Those who are nearest and dearest to us, those whom we trust with our happiness and our good name, may become traitors to their faith. The money that a man has, he may lose. It flies away from him, perhaps when he needs it the most. A man's reputation may be sacrificed in a moment of ill-considered action. The people who are prone to fall on their knees to do us honor when success is with us may be the first to throw the stone of malice when failure settles its cloud upon our heads. The one absolutely unselfish friend that a man can have in this selfish world, the one that never deserts him

9

and the one that never proves ungrateful or treacherous, is his dog.

Gentlemen of the Jury, a man's dog stands by him in prosperity and in poverty, in health and sickness. He will sleep on the cold ground, where the wintry winds blow and the snow drives fiercely, if only he may be near his master's side. He will kiss the hand that has no food to offer, he will lick the wounds and sores that come in encounters with the roughness of the world. He guards the sleep of his pauper master as if he were a prince. When all other friends desert he remains. When riches take wings and reputation falls to pieces, he is as constant in his love as the sun in its journey through the heavens. If fortune drives the master forth an outcast in the world, friendless and homeless, the faithful dog asks no higher privilege than that of accompanying him to guard against danger, to fight against his enemies, and when the last scene of all comes, and death takes the master in its embrace and his body is laid away in the cold ground, no matter if all other friends pursue their way, there by his graveside will the noble dog be found, his head between his paws, his eyes sad but open in alert watchfulness, faithful and true even to death."

An Answer To Byron's Eulogy To a Dog

In the 1870's there lived in Wyoming County, West Virginia, two respectable citizens, Grandville Moxley and Hiram Clay. Moxley's hound dog bit Clay's daughter and Clay killed the dog. Moxley brought suit for the damages. This turned out to be one of the most interesting cases ever held in the county.

Colonel Milton French and Captain William Walker represented Moxley, and Major J. H. (Fud) McGinnis, represented Clay.

During the argument Colonel French quoted Byron's Eulogy to a Dog, after which Major McGinnis arose and made his plea closing with the following poem:

> Grandville Moxley once had a hound,
>   Now he is lost and can't be found,
> But somewhere in the desert wild,
>   He rests beneath his funeral pyre.
>
> So let the ravens soaring high,
>   Toll his dishonored yelping cry,
> And let the roaming foxes smile,
>   Passing the brute that bit the child.
>
> Yes, let him rest in deep disgrace,
>   Leave not a stone to mark the place;

11

Now show the plaintiff in this suit,
  You favor not this vicious brute.

Now gentlemen, I've said to you,
  What I believe you ought to do,
Go to your room, return and say
  We find no guilt in Hiram Clay.

The jury's verdict was in favor of Clay.

The Law
and
Your Dog

1

History of Canine Law

As "Man's Best Friend," dogs have not faired very well, legally speaking. Until the various states began to enact dog laws, the common-law concept of Blackstone was the main source. In the eyes of the common law the dog was a base and inferior kind of an animal and entitled to very little protection. Blackstone and the courts list three things that made the dog inferior to other domestic animals: (1) They do not serve as food; (2) They originally belonged to a class of wild animals that are subject to distressing and incurable diseases which they communicate to animals and humans by their bite; (3) They are kept for purposes which require them to keep some of their natural ferocity, and as a result they are liable to injure property and humans. Good examples of canine jurisprudence in the United States under the common law are found in the following discussions:

In one of the two cases the Supreme Court of the United States has decided involving dogs, Justice Brown wrote in 1896 in *Sentell vs. New Orleans*, 166 U.S. 698, 17 S.Ct. 693:

15

The very fact that they (dogs) are without the protection of the criminal law shows that property in dogs is of an imperfect or qualified nature, and that they stand, as it were, between animals ferae naturae in which, until killed or subdued, there is no property, and domestic animals, in which the rights of property is perfect and complete. They are not considered as being upon the same plane with horses, cattle, sheep and other domesticated animals, but rather in the category of cats, monkeys, parrots, singing birds and similar animals kept for pleasure, curiosity or caprice. They have no intrinsic value, by which we understand a value common to all dogs as such, and independent of the particular breed or individual. Unlike other domestic animals, they are useful neither as beasts of burden, for draught (except to a limited extent), nor for food. They are peculiar in the fact that they differ among themselves more widely than any other class of animals, and can hardly be said to have a characteristic common to the entire race. While the higher breeds rank among the noblest representatives of the animal kingdom, and are justly esteemed for their intelligence, sagacity, fidelity, watchfulness, affection, and, above all, for their natural companionship with man, others are afflicted with such serious infirmities of temper as to be little better than a public nuisance. All are more or less subject to attack of hydrophobic madness.

In the above case the owner of a Newfoundland bitch, registered in the American Kennel's stud book and kept by the owner for breeding purposes, was attempting to recover damages for the loss of his dog, who had been killed on a railroad track. A statute provided that no dog be entitled to the protection of the law unless placed upon the assessment rolls, and that no recovery for its value can be had for more than the amount fixed by the owner in the last assessment. The Court held that the statute is a constitutional exercise of the police power and denied the owner recovery because he had not complied with the statute. The Court said, "Although dogs are ordinarily harmless, they preserve some of their hereditary wolfish instincts, which occasionally break forth in the destruction of sheep and other animals. Others, too small to attack these animals, are simply vicious, noisy and pestilent."

In the only other case, *Nicchia vs. People of New York*, 154 U.S. 228, decided in 1920, the Supreme Court quoted the *Sentell* case with approval. Lillian Nicchia owned two dogs in New York City and refused to obtain a license as required by law. She was convicted and fined. The Court held that property in dogs is of an imperfect or qualified nature, and they may be subjected to peculiar and drastic police regulations by the state without depriving their owner of any federal rights.

The state courts in the early beginning followed the common-law concept. Dogs were held to be of no intrinsic value; and so they were not subject to laws governing larceny, but were considered an inferior sort of property in which the owner's rights could be enforced by civil proceedings.

The courts very early defined "animal" as a creature "which is not human, endowed with power of voluntary motion." They attempted to judicially classify animals in two classes, wild or *ferae naturae*, and domestic or *domitae naturae*. A further division was made between animals that were regarded as being by nature generous or base and not subject to larceny.

Thus those animals that did not serve mankind for food but were kept for "mere whim or pleasure of the

owner" were in the eyes of the law of no intrinsic value.
There are many cases reported involving "Man's Best
Friend." In rendering opinions judges seem to be fond
of quoting poetry and folklore about the dog as the friend
of the poor and the protector of the weak.

A judge in the early case of *McCallister vs. Sapping-
field*, 144 P. 142 (1914) said, "We find that poetry and
history have been cited in his (dog's) behalf and his
achievements recounted in glowing languages; this concept being caught up by the immortal bard who sang:

> "But the poor dog, in life the firmest friend,
> The first to welcome, foremost to defend,
> Whose honest heart is still his Master's own,
> Who labors, fights, lives, breathes for him alone,
> Unhonour'd falls, unnoticed all his worth,
> Denied in Heaven the soul be held on earth,
> While man, vain insect, hopes to be forgiven,
> And claims himself as sole exclusive heaven."

Yet some courts seemed bent on painting the dog as
carnivorous beast, ferocious and dangerous.

At common law a person could not be convicted of
stealing a dog, but the owner could bring a civil action
against someone who killed or injured the animal. A Virginia case explains this early theory by saying, "As to
all other animals which do not serve for food, such as
dogs and ferrets, though tame and salable, or other crea-
tures kept for whim or pleasure, stealing these does not
amount to larceny at common law. By common law the
property in dogs and other inferior animals is not such
as that larceny can be committed by stealing them, though
the possessor has a base property in them, and may maintain a civil action for injury done."

The rule of the common law was technical in the extreme: while it was not larceny to steal a dog while living, it was larceny to steal his hide after he was dead. It is easy to understand why the early law books said that "dog law" was as hard to define as was "dog Latin."

But that day has passed and dogs have now a distinct and well-established status in the eyes of the law. A good case to show how the Courts began to change their thinking is *Vaughn v. Nelson*, 62 S.E. 708, decided in 1908 by the Supreme Court of Georgia.

Nelson sued out an attachment to recover the purchase price of a dog described as "one white and liver and ticked pointer bitch named Maude." Vaughn filed a claim setting up that the dog was not property under the laws of Georgia, and was not liable to attachment, levy, and sale. The trial judge ruled that the dog was so subject. On appeal to the Supreme Court of Georgia the Court upheld the trial court saying:

"We are of the opinion that the rule of the judge of the Superior Court was correct, and that dogs are as much the subject of property right as are other domestic animals, and therefore, as property, may be levied on and sold. In the evolution of dogology, it is a matter of common knowledge that dogs now have a market value, and that many persons earn a livelihood by either raising, buying, selling, training, or exhibiting dogs."

The Court then referred to the Jamison case, where the Court had held that dogs had no market value, and the same rules of damages that were applicable in the case of livestock killed by the running of trains could not be applied to them. The Court explained the decision by saying: "It is clear that the decision in the *Jamison* case resulted from judicial notice of what was perhaps at that time (1885) the fact that dogs had no market value."

Citing *Graham vs. Smith*, 100 Ga. 434, 28 S.E. 225, the Court said, "The judgment of the Superior Court, holding that the owner of a dog had such property in it as would enable him to maintain an action in trover for its recovery was affirmed, was authority that dogs do have market value and are property."

The Court then stated that, "The decision in the *Graham* case was the first step toward adjusting the law to the changed condition of affairs with regard to dogs as property of value; and this was followed as a matter of judicial history.

"The writer [Judge] is not prepared to bemoan the evil associations and untimely death of old Troy, and has but little association with Fido or Trip, and therefore can take but little part in the settlement of the question raised by the briefs as to the value of the faithful watchdog as a boon of priceless worth, nor is he prepared to give his sanction to the maledictions pronounced upon the worthless cur. We leave those views of the subject to abler pens. If one is interested in the dog pensive, watchful, mythological, historic, or philosophic, he will find all phases of this many sided animal portrayed in the opinion of Judge Lumpkin of the Atlanta Circuit, as quoted by Judge Cobb in the Strong case. We view the dog only from the standpoint of the well-organized fact, to which we cannot shut our eyes, that he is daily bought and sold, raised for profit, trained for profit, exhibited for profit. He may not bear burdens like the famous Flemish dogs of Holland, and draw the peddlers' heavy carts described by Onida, until his withers are unstrung and he drops fainting by the wayside. He may not be valuable as a draft horse. But that he may have value, be it much or little and therefore must be property, is well evidenced by the facts of this case. The attachment was taken out for the purchase price of the dog, showing that he was originally sold. He was claimed by the defendant in error, which implied value, and when sold under judicial process, which is attacked as null and void for the reason that a canine cannot be of value, he again brought, even upon the block, a 'fancy' figure. For authority in other jurisdictions holding that the dog is property, see *Mullaly v. People*, 86 N.Y. 365, in which it is said: "Large amounts of money are now invested in dogs, and they are largely the subject of trade and traffic. In many ways they are put to useful service, and, so far as pertains to their ownership as personal property, they possess all the attributes of other personal property." In Michigan "dogs have value and are the property of their owner, as much as any other animal which one may have or keep." *Ten Hopen v. Walker*, 96 Mich. 236, 55 N. W. 657, 35 Am. St. Rep. 598. In *Lynn v. State*, 33 Tex. Cr. R. 153, 25 S. W. 779, it is held that a homicide even may be justified in the possession or protection of a dog by its owner. There is diversity of opinions and conflict of authority among the courts of different states as to whether a dog can be killed in the exercise of police power, and the owner thus be deprived of his dog without a trial of his right of property guaranteed by the Constitution, but it cannot seriously be questioned that the owner may maintain trover, replevin, or trespass against anyone taking his dog and converting it to his own use. Many of the decisions holding that a dog is not property are based upon the character of the dog, and the assumption that he is an animal *ferae naturae*. The Supreme Court of this state, however, in *Wilcox v. State*, 101 Ga. 563, 28 S. E. 981, 39 L. R. A. 709, held that a dog was classed in the Constitution of this state as a domestic animal; and this ruling was distinctly reiterated in the *Strong* Case, supra. Not only was the dog property under the common law, but in New York, Kansas, Texas, North Carolina, Indiana, New Hampshire, Michigan, Massachusetts, and Missouri dogs have been held to be the subject of property right.

Following the rational trend of modern authority, we are compelled to hold that in Georgia a dog, whether he be a remote descendant of the small spaniel who changed the current of modern history by saving the life of William of Orange, or carries in his veins the blood of the faithful St. Bernard who rescues the lost traveler from the stormswept crest of the beetling Alps, may be sold in this state to satisfy even the humblest debt of his owner.

An extract from an opinion of a judge in 1903 indicates the length a judge will go to prove man's best friend should be man's property in the eyes of the law.

The dog has figured very extensively in the past and present. In mythology, as Cerberus, he was intrusted with watching the gates of hell, and he seems to have performed his duties so well that there were but few escapes. In the history of the past, he has been used extensively for hunting purposes, as the guardian of persons and property, and as a pet and companion. He is the much valued possession of hunters the world over, and in England especially is the pack o' hounds highly prized. In literature he has appeared more often than any other animal, except perhaps the horse. Sometimes he is greatly praised, and at others greatly abused. Sometimes he is made the type of what is mean, low, and contemptible; while at others he is described in terms of eulogy. Few men will forget the song of their childhood, which runs:

"Old dog Tray's ever faithful;
Grief cannot drive him away;
He is gentle, he is kind;
I'll never, never find
A better friend than old dog Tray."

Nor can any of us fail to remember the intelligent animal on whose behalf "Old Mother Hubbard went to the cupboard."

Few men have deserved, and few have won, higher praise in an epitaph than the following, which was written by Lord Byron in regard to his dead Newfoundland: "Near this spot are deposited the remains of one who possessed beauty without vanity, ferocity, and all the virtues of man without his vices. This praise, which would be unmeaning flattery if inscribed over human ashes, is but a just tribute to the memory of Boatswain, a dog who was born at Newfoundland May 3, 1803, and died at Newstead Abbey November 18, 1808." The dog has even invaded the domain of art. All who have seen Sir Edwin Landseer's great pictures will know how much human intelligence can be expressed in the face of a dog. His picture entitled "Laying Down the Law" will not be forgotten in considering the dog as a litigant. Thus the dog has figured in mythology, history, poetry, fiction, and art from the earliest times down to the present, and now in these closing days of the nineteenth century we are called upon to decide whether a dog is a wild animal (ferae naturae) in such sense as not to be leviable property; or, if he is a domestic animal (domitae naturae), whether he is not subject to levy, on the ancient theory that he had no intrinsic value if he was not good to eat. Originally, all the animals which are now used by man were wild. One after another they have become domesticated, and subject to his control, ownership, and use. As time progressed, they gradually lost their character of wildness, and became more and more subject to mankind, and more and more regarded as ordinary property. At this day no one would contend that the horse was not the subject of absolute property because his ancestors were originally wild, and the same may be said of other animals now thoroughly recognized as domestic. Even in the days of Blackstone, while it was declared that the property in a dog was "base property," it was nevertheless asserted that such property was sufficient to maintain a civil action for its loss. 4 Bl. Com. 236. Since that day, in the evolution of civilization, the dog has not been left behind. He is now not only prized for hunting purposes, as a watchdog, and as a pet; but it is common knowledge that many dogs have an actual commercial and market value. When annually there is held in New York a bench show, at which dogs take prizes amounting to thousands of dollars, and where they are bought and sold at prices which are frequently far larger than are paid for ordinary horses, it is rather late in the day to assert they are not valuable property. Dogs are also trained for purposes of exhibition, being sometimes the sole means of support of their masters. It would be an interesting survival of archaic law to say that a showman could put up his tent, give nightly exhibitions of his valuable dogs, making large sums of money from them, get in debt to any given extent, laugh at his creditors, and proceed with his daily exhibitions, on the ground that his stock in trade is not subject to levy. If it be contended that the horse, mule, and other animals are used for more practical purposes, some of them as beasts of burden, it need only be asked what animals draw the sleds of the Eskimos and others in the Northern latitudes? Nor is this confined alone to the Arctic Regions. Any traveler on the continent of Europe, and especially through Belgium, who has kept his eyes open, has seen these animals drawing heavy loads, and often taking the place of other draft animals. To indulge in technical refinement, and declare that the dog is not subject to levy, although he belongs to a debtor, is useful to him, can be and is actually used, may be transferred by him to another, and is as much the subject of bargain and sale as any other property, merely because in the remote past the ownership of his progenitors may have been considered qualified or "base," seems to me untenable on its face. The ancient idea that "animals which do not serve for food, and which therefore the law holds to have no intrinsic value," were not the subject of larceny (4 Bl. Com. 236), has passed away. Now the stomach is not the only criterion of value. Even then, as already stated, a civil action could be brought for the loss of a dog. Generally, property which may be sold and possession delivered is a subject of levy, omitting choses in action and equitable assets. 7 Am. & Eng. Enc. L. 127.

The dog has been very often before the courts of the different states and of different countries, and has been the subject of a good deal of judicial humor and judicial learning; but it bears a tinge of the ridiculous to contend that, however many and however valuable dogs a man may own, he cannot be made to pay his debts if he will only invest his money in dogs—a contention which reminds one of the very solemn discussions in a certain court, at a time not very long past, as to whether the oyster was a wild animal. Before the courts, the dog has received a treatment as varied as that given him by authors. As illustrative of the widely different light in which judges have viewed him, I cite only one or two cases. Monroe, J., in *Wilson v. Railroad Co.*, 10 Rich. (S. C.) 52, indulged in some vituperative epithets upon a poor canine who was so unfortunate as to be run over by a railroad train. On the other hand, in the case of *State v. Harriman*, 75 Me. 562, 46 Am. Rep. 423, in which a majority of the court held that dogs did not fall within the criminal statute of that state against the killing or wounding of "domestic animals," Appleton, C. J., dissented most vigorously, making use of the following language, as quoted by the Supreme Court of Georgia in *Patton v. State*, 93 Ga. 112, 19 S. E. 734, 24 L. R. A. 732: "He is a domestic animal. From the time of the pyramids to the present day; from the frozen pole to the torrid zone—wherever man has been —there has been his dog. Cuvier has asserted that the dog was, perhaps, necessary for the establishment of civilized society, and that a little reflection will convince us that barbarous nations owe much of their civilization above the brute to the possession of the dog. He is the friend and companion of his master, accompanying him in his walks; his servant, aiding him in his hunting; the playmate of his children; an inmate of his house, protecting it against all assailants."

I need not stop to discuss the learned dog law evolved by judges of other states and countries. Turning to our own state, I will only glance hastily at the status of our law with reference to the dog. At the outset, I may remark that the argument used with reference to dogs applies much more strongly to some other animals and to birds. It will be readily perceived that lions, tigers, and other wild animals which are captured, and reduced from their native state to the subjection of the menagerie, are much less domestic animals, or animals in which there is absolute property, than dogs. So, likewise, birds which are entrapped and kept in cages are much nearer their wild state than the dog; and yet it will hardly be contended that all the traveling menageries of the country are free from levy, or that a man may set up an aviary, and make an excellent living by selling birds, while his sorrowing creditors hang about his door with a bailiff and a fi. fa., but can come no nearer to the desideratum of a levy than to "listen to the mocking bird.

With the beginning of the twentieth century the courts and the legislatures were forced to begin changing the laws as to dogs and recognizing that they do have value; they are property just as much as horses, cattle and automobiles, and they are a source of taxation. Therefore, the modern concept is that they are personal property and can be subject of larceny. To determine the elements of larceny necessary for a conviction for stealing a dog, one must consult the statutory laws of the particular state.

In August 1966 our United States Congress passed for the first time a law pertaining to dogs: an act to protect dogs, cats and other animals intended for research or experimental use. The Secretary of Agriculture is authorized to regulate the transportation, sale and handling of dogs, cats and certain other animals intended to be used for research or experimental use. The act also requires a person, firm or corporation to obtain a license from the Secretary of Agriculture before dealing in the sale or transportation of dogs, cats and other animals intended to be used for research. Research facilities are required to register with the Secretary of Agriculture. The act provides as follows:

An act to authorize the Secretary of Agriculture to regulate the transportation, sale, and handling of dogs, cats, and certain other animals intended to be used for purpose of research or experimentation, and for other purposes. Dogs, cats and other animals intended for research or experimental use.

Be it enacted by the Senate and House of Representatives of the United States of America in Congress assembled, That in order to protect the owners of dogs and cats from theft of such pets, to prevent the sale or use of dogs and cats which have been stolen, and to insure that certain animals intended for use in research facilities are provided humane care and treatment, it is essential to regulate the transportation, purchase, sale, housing, care, handling, and treatment of such animals by persons or organizations engaged in using them for research or experimental purposes or in transportation, buying, or selling them for such use.

DEFINITIONS

SEC. 2. When used in this Act—

(a) The term "person" includes any individual, partnership, firm, joint stock company, corporation, associations, trust, estate, or other legal entity;

(b) The term "Secretary" means the Secretary of Agriculture;

(c) The term "commerce" means commerce between any State, territory, or possession, or the District of Columbia, or the Commonwealth of Puerto Rico, and any place outside thereof; or between points within the same State, territory, or possession, or the District of Columbia, or the Commonwealth of Puerto Rico, but through any place outside thereof; or within any territory, possession, or the District of Columbia;

(d) The term "dog" means any live dog (Canis familiaris);

(e) The term "cat" means any live cat (Felis catus);

(f) The term "research facility" means any school, institution, organization, or person, that uses or intends to use dogs or cats in research, tests, or experiments, and that (1) purchases or transports dogs or cats in commerce, or (2) receives funds under a grant, award, loan, or contract from a department, agency, or instrumentality of the United States for the purpose of carrying out research, tests, or experiments;

(g) The term "dealer" means any person who for compensation or profit delivers for transportation, or transports, except as a common carrier, buys, or sells dogs or cats in commerce for research purposes;

(h) The term "animal" means live dogs, cats, monkeys (nonhuman primate mammals), guinea pigs, hamsters, and rabbits.

LICENSES TO DEALERS

SEC. 3. The Secretary shall issue licenses to dealers upon application therefor in such form and manner as he may prescribe and upon payment of such fee established pursuant to section 23 of this act: *Provided,* That no such license shall be issued until the dealer shall have demonstrated that his facilities comply with the standards promulgated by the Secretary pursuant to section 13 of this Act: *Provided, however,* That any person who derives less than a substantial portion of his income (as determined by the Secretary) from the breeding and raising of dogs or cats on his own premises and sells any such dog or cat to a dealer or research facility shall not be required to obtain a license as a dealer under this Act. The Secretary is further authorized to license, as dealers, persons who do not qualify as dealers within the meaning of this Act upon such persons' complying with the requirements specified above and agreeing, in writing, to comply with all the requirements of this Act and the regulations promulgated by the Secretary hereunder.

LICENSE REQUIREMENT

SEC. 4. No dealer shall sell or offer to sell or transport or offer for transportation to any research facility any dog or cat, or buy, sell, offer to buy or sell, transport or offer for transportation in commerce to or from another dealer under this Act any dog or cat, unless and until such dealer shall have obtained a license from the Secretary and such license shall not have been suspended or revoked.

SEC. 5. No dealer shall sell or otherwise dispose of any dog or cat within a period of five business days after the acquisition of such animal or within such other period as may be specified by the Secretary.

REGISTRATION

SEC. 6. Every research facility shall register with the Secretary in accordance with such rules and regulations as he may prescribe.

PURCHASE RESTRICTIONS

SEC. 7. It shall be unlawful for any research facility to purchase any dog or cat from any person except a person holding a valid license as a dealer issued by the Secretary pursuant to this Act unless such person is exempted from obtaining such license under Section 3 of this Act.

TRANSACTIONS BY U. S. AGENCIES

SEC. 8. No department, agency, or instrumentality of the United States which uses animals for research or experimentation shall purchase or otherwise acquire any dog or cat for such purposes from any person except a person holding a valid license as a dealer issued by the Secretary pursuant to this Act unless such person

is exempted from obtaining such license under Section 3 of this Act.

ENFORCEMENT

SEC. 9. When construing or enforcing the provisions of this Act, the act, omission, or failure of any individual acting for or employed by a research facility or a dealer, or a person licensed as a dealer pursuant to the second sentence of section 3, within the scope of his employment or office, shall be deemed the act, omission, or failure of such research facility, dealer, or other person as well as of such individual.

RECORDKEEPING

SEC. 10. Research facilities and dealers shall make, and retain for such reasonable period of time as the Secretary may prescribe, such records with respect to the purchase, sale, transportation, identification, and previous ownership of dogs and cats but not monkeys, guinea pigs, hamsters, or rabbits as the Secretary may prescribe, upon forms supplied by the Secretary. Such records shall be made available at all reasonable times for inspection by the Secretary, by any Federal officer or employee designated by the Secretary.

IDENTIFICATION

SEC. 11. All dogs and cats delivered for transportation, transported, purchased, or sold in commerce by any dealer shall be marked or identified at such time and in such humane manner as the Secretary may prescribe.

HUMANE STANDARDS PROMULGATION

SEC. 12. The Secretary is authorized to promulgate humane standards and recordkeeping requirements governing the purchase, handling, or sale of dogs or cats by dealers or research facilities at auction sales.

SEC. 13. The Secretary shall establish and promulgate standards to govern the humane handling, care, treatment, and transportation of animals by dealers and research facilities. Such standards shall include minimum requirements with respect to the housing, feeding, watering, sanitation, ventilation, shelter from extremes of weather and temperature, separation by species, and adequate veterinary care. The foregoing shall not be construed as authorizing the Secretary to prescribe standards for the handling, care, or treatment of animals during actual research or experimentation by a research facility as determined by such research facility.

COMPLIANCE BY U.S. AGENCIES

SEC. 14. Any department, agency, or instrumentality of the United States having laboratory animal facilities shall comply with the standards promulgated by the Secretary for a research facility under section 13.

SEC. 15. (a) The Secretary shall consult and cooperate with other Federal departments, agencies, or instrumentalities concerned with the welfare of animals used for research or experimentation when establishing standards pursuant to section 13 and in carrying out the purposes of this Act.

(b) The Secretary is authorized to cooperate with the officials of the various States or political subdivisions thereof in effectuating the purposes of this Act and of any State, local, or municipal legislation or ordinance on the same subject.

INVESTIGATION OR INSPECTIONS

SEC. 16. The Secretary shall make such investigations or inspections as he deems necessary to determine whether any dealer or research facility has violated or is violating any provision of this Act or any regulation issued thereunder. The Secretary shall promulgate such rules and regulations as he deems necessary to permit

inspectors to confiscate or destroy in a humane manner any animals found to be suffering as a result of a failure to comply with any provision of this Act or any regulation issued thereunder if (1) such animals are held by a dealer, or (2) such animals are held by a research facility and are no longer required by such research facility to carry out the research, test, or experiment for which such animals have been utilized.

SEC. 17. The Secretary shall issue rules and regulations requiring licensed dealers and research facilities to permit inspection of their animals and records at reasonable hours upon request by legally constituted law enforcement agencies in search of lost animals.

SEC. 18. Nothing in this Act shall be construed as authorizing the Secretary to promulgate rules, regulations, or orders for the handling, care, treatment, or inspection of animals during actual research or experimentation by a research facility as determined as such research facility.

SUSPENSION OR DEALER'S LICENSE

SEC. 19. (a) If the Secretary has reason to believe that any person licensed as a dealer has violated or is violating any provision of this Act or any of the rules or regulations promulgated by the Secretary hereunder, the Secretary may suspend such person's license temporarily, but not to exceed twenty-one days, and, after notice and opportunity for hearing, may suspend for such additional period as he may specify or revoke such license, if such violation is determined to have occurred and may make an order that such person shall cease and desist from continuing such violation.

JUDICIAL REVIEW

(b) Any dealer aggrieved by a final order of the Secretary issued pursuant to subsection (a) of this section may, within sixty days after entry of such an order,

seek review of such order in the manner provided in section 10 of the administrative Procedure Act (5 U.S.C. 1009).

(c) Any dealer who violates any provision of this Act shall, on conviction thereof, be subject to imprisonment for not more than one year or a fine of not more than $1,000, or both.

VIOLATIONS BY RESEARCH FACILITIES: PENALTY

SEC. 20. (a) If the Secretary has reason to believe that any research facility has violated or is violating any provision of this Act or any of the rules or regulations promulgated by the Secretary hereunder and if, after notice and opportunity for hearing, he finds a violation, he may make an order that such research facility shall cease and desist from continuing such violation. Such cease and desist order shall become effective fifteen days after issuance of the order. Any research facility which knowingly fails to obey a cease-and-desist order made by the Secretary under this section shall be subject to a civil penalty of $500 for each offense, and each day during which such failure continues shall be deemed a separate offense.

JUDICIAL REVIEW

(b) Any research facility aggrieved by a final order of the Secretary issued pursuant to subsection (a) of this section may, within sixty days after entry of such order, seek review of such order in the district court for the district in which such research facility is located in the manner provided in section 10 of the Administrative Procedure Act (U.S.C. 1009).

RULES AND REGULATIONS

SEC. 21. The Secretary is authorized to promulgate such rules, regulations, and orders as he may deem necessary in order to effectuate the purposes of this Act.

SEC. 22. If any provision of this Act or the applica-

tion of any such provision to any person or circumstances shall be held invalid, the remainder of this Act and the application of any such provision to persons or circumstances other than those as to which it is held invalid shall not be affected thereby.

LICENSE FEES: APPROPRIATION

SEC. 23. The Secretary shall charge, assess, and cause to be collected reasonable fees for licenses issued. Such fees shall be adjusted on an equitable basis taking into consideration the type and nature of the operations to be licensed and shall be deposited and covered into the Treasury as miscellaneous receipts. There are hereby authorized to be appropriated such funds as Congress may from time to time provide.

APPROPRIATION

EFFECTIVE DATES

SEC. 24. The regulations referred to in section 10 and section 13 shall be prescribed by the Secretary as soon as reasonable but not later than six months from the date of enactment of this Act. Additions and amendments thereto may be prescribed from time to time as may be necessary or advisable. Compliance by dealers with the provisions of this Act and such regulations shall commence ninety days after the promulgation of such regulations. Compliance by research facilities with the provisions of this Act and such regulations shall commence six months after the promulgation of such regulations, except that the Secretary may grant extensions of time to research facilities which do not comply with the standards prescribed by the Secretary pursuant to section 13 of this Act provided that the Secretary determines that there is evidence that the research facilities will meet such standards within a reasonable time.

"Approved August 24, 1966."

2

Licenses and Regulations

General:

It is well recognized by all the states that the legislature of each state, under the police power, may regulate the use of animals of all kinds. Local legislative bodies such as municipal corporations may by ordinance regulate the keeping and use of animals within the city limits. Of course, this power cannot be unreasonable or arbitrary. The courts uphold such regulations on the grounds that it is for the common good and protection of the community. The police power has been exercised to regulate and control dogs more often than any other animal. (This is based on the theory that laws are enacted for the greatest good to the greatest number of people.) This is the same basis for public health laws and regulations. The laws are not limited to dogs running at large but extend to the right of keeping dogs. Since dogs are personal property, they come within the provisions of the Constitution against taking property without due process.

Since each state has the power to license and regulate

dogs within its boundary, the owner of a dog must consult the statutory law of the state and the city ordinances of the city where he is keeping his dog in order to determine the nature and extent of licenses, taxes and regulations. In this chapter it can only be pointed out the general outline states and cities take in regulating dogs.

Licenses:

The fees charged for licenses are considered a controlling method rather than purely a tax. The right to own or keep a dog is made possible by requiring the owner to obtain a license and pay a fee. It is much like an automobile license. The license itself does not denote ownership, but a privilege or a right to possess and have the animal for the owner's own use and enjoyment. It is a license that must be obtained each year, and it is not transferable from one owner of a dog to another who might purchase the dog, nor is it transferable from dog to dog. The courts have upheld the right of the government to require licenses for dogs, as well as certain other personal property, even to the point that the license fee does not have to be uniform and equal. The fact a higher license fee is required for female dogs than for male dogs does not make the statute or ordinance unconstitutional.

In the case of *State v. Anderson*, 234 S.W. 768 (1920), the court set forth the licensing theory as related to dogs: "We do not think that the imposition of a license fee as a condition precedent to the right of citizens of this state to own or keep a dog under the terms and purposes of the statute involved is the levying of a tax under the state's taxing powers, but is a method adopted by the

Legislature of regulating the keeping of a dog. There is a marked distinction between taxation for revenue and the imposing of license fees for the purpose of regulations in the exercise of the police power of the state." Most of the states hold that an imposition of a license fee for the keeping of dogs is not a tax, but is merely a fee for the purpose of regulation.

The amount of the license fee varies from state to state and city to city. Generally the fee for the female is higher than for the male. Each state provides for a minimum age requirement before a dog is required to have a license— generally from three to six months.

Licenses are issued annually. Double licensing is permitted. State, city and county may require the owner or keeper of a dog to acquire a license.

Kennel licenses may be obtained in many states and cities. Each kennel license permits the owner to have a certain number of dogs, with an additional charge for each dog over the maximum permitted.

As seen above, regulations involving dogs may be by licensing or it may be through the police power of the state. But regardless of the method used, the law can be very strict, and generally the dog owner is treated very harshly. The laws of each state differ, but the regulations generally fall into a pattern.

The strict laws whereby a dog may be killed when roaming upon another's premises unaccompanied by his owner have been held constitutional. Ohio passed in 1965 what has been described as the strictest leash law in the United States. All dogs must be on a leash, tied, or fenced in 24 hours a day. It provides:

It shall be unlawful for the owner, keeper or harborer of any female dog to permit such dog to go beyond the premises of such owner or keeper at any time such dog is in heat, unless such dog is properly in leash.

The owner or keeper of every dog shall at all times keep such dog either confined upon the premises of the owner or firmly secured by means of a collar and chain or other device so that it cannot stray beyond the premises of the owner or keeper, or it shall be kept under reasonable control of some person, except when lawfully engaged in hunting accompanied by an owner or handler.

A large number of states merely require that dogs must wear a collar and license tag attached to the collar when off the premises of the owner or keeper.

Most cities require dogs to be on a leash when off the owner's premises and muzzled when on the public streets alone. The courts have held such muzzling ordinance valid but held that provisions for shooting such dog are invalid.

In the case of *King v. Arlington County*, 81 S.E.(2) 587 (Va.), the Court held that the county ordinance which provided: "It shall be unlawful for any person to keep within the county of Arlington any dog which is known to be vicious or which has evidenced a disposition to attack human beings" a valid ordinance. The Court said: "Clearly, we think, the prohibition against keeping a dog which is known to be vicious or which has evidenced a disposition to attack human beings, is within this grant of police power."

Statutes authorizing a humane society to seize unlicensed dogs and to destroy or otherwise dispose of those not redeemed within a stated number of days after seizure are a part of the regulations authorized to control dogs under the police power.

Zoning:

Zoning is just another method of controlling dogs. Generally speaking, zoning laws do not involve the owner of one or two dogs kept as pets. But once the owner is found raising a litter of puppies he may be in violation of the zoning laws. The violation comes about under the section defining a kennel. Zoning laws may define a kennel as a place where more than four dogs are kept. The number of dogs may vary and an examination of the local zoning laws will disclose the definition of a kennel. A typical zoning regulation states that anyone having more than four dogs must obtain a special-use permit and that such kennelling must be conducted within a building so constructed that no noise of any kind produced therein shall be audible beyond the confines of the building. The fact that the owner occasionally raises a litter of puppies and is doing so as a hobby is not protection.

Zoning authorities have written the regulations in such a way that many dog owners are beginning to rebel and demand reasonable canine legislation. Such is the case in Kentucky, which now permits the occasional raising of a litter and occasional sale of puppies under the Miller Act.

Boarding and commercial kennels and animal hospitals are not permitted in areas zoned for residential purposes only. Local business and commercial areas generally permit kennels. Before attempting to establish a commercial

or boarding kennel or an animal hospital in any area it
is wise to check the zoning laws.

Dogs as a Nuisance:

The question of whether a dog constitutes a nuisance
depends upon the manner in which it is kept. Generally,
it has been held that a dog is not a nuisance *per se*. That
is, it is not a nuisance in itself or inherently a nuisance.
The mere fact that a person is keeping a dog does not constitute a nuisance. To be a nuisance, the owner or keeper
of a dog allows it to act in such a manner that it becomes a
menace to health or prevents another from the reasonable
and comfortable use of his property. A nuisance may be
constituted by the owner's failing to keep the dogs clean
or by needless barking or in some manner causing the
neighbor annoyance to a degree that he cannot enjoy his
property.

A good example of such a case is *Krebs v. Hermann*,
6 P.(2) 907. A veterinarian surgeon owned and operated
a dog hospital where he treated and cared for sick and
injured dogs. He also bought and sold the animals. A
neighbor, who lived within 45 feet of the hospital and
kennel, asked for an injunction prohibiting the veterinarian from operating his kennel and hospital on the
grounds that it was a nuisance. The veterinarian claimed
that he had built his building first and therefore he was
entitled to operate his business. The Court held that the
law does not give the owner of a building the right to
maintain a nuisance in it merely because he constructed
the same before other buildings were constructed and

later occupied by persons who have been injured by the nuisance conducted in the building first erected. The keeping of from forty to eighty dogs, from whose kennels offensive odors arise, and whose barking in the nighttime when aroused by the passing of automobiles on a much-travelled highway breaks the rest of persons living on adjoining premises, is a private nuisance. Injunctive relief against a private nuisance will not be denied because great financial loss would result to the one causing the nuisance.

Whether the keeping of a dog or dogs is a nuisance is a question of facts of each particular case. The burden of proving a nuisance rests upon the person who complains.

3

Ownership and Sale

The Romans considered all animals *ferae naturae*, as common property and having no owner. The title to animals was vested in the sovereign as a personal prerogative. In the early history of England the common law held that animals belonged to the Crown. The law began to change with the Charter of the Forest by Henry III in 1225 when the rights of the King to unreclaimed wild animals were limited. The rule of law recognizing the qualified title of the Crown to wild animals became the common law of the United States, and as we have seen in Chapter 1, governments gradually changed the concept of ownership of dogs from a wild animal, to property of an inferior sort, to the modern concept of valuable personal property. Therefore, ownership is acquired in the same manner as other personal property—by possession. Actual transfer of possession is when the owner agrees to give up all rights and possession to the dog. Implied transfer is where the owner agrees to keep actual possession of the dog for a certain length of time or until the new owner requests the actual possession.

Sale and transfer of dogs is controlled by the same

43

laws that govern the sale of personal property. A sale has been defined as the transfer of ownership for a valuable consideration. It is a contract founded on a valuable consideration by which the property is transferred from the seller to the buyer. A contract of sale is where the owner of a dog signifies his willingness to sell and another person signifies his willingness to buy the dog for a specified price. The courts often speak of the "meeting of the minds" in dealing with contracts of sale. To have a binding contract there must be a meeting of the minds on all important elements involved in the contract. The agreement must include the particular dog, the price, and the time and place of delivery. In a recent decision the court said, "an acceptance, to be effectual, must be identical with the offer in all material points and unconditional; prior to unconditional acceptance of the offer the offer may be withdrawn."

Thus, when an owner of a dog states in a letter to another that he will sell a certain dog at a certain price, and asks the purchaser to wire or write stating if he desires to purchase the dog, and the purchaser sends a letter stating that he agrees to purchase the dog at the price stated, a binding contract now exists. When an offer is made the acceptance, to be binding, must be identical with the offer and it must be unconditional. The seller is at liberty to withdraw his offer to sell at any time prior to the buyer's accepting his offer.

The contract of sale may be in writing, it may be oral, or it may be an implied contract from the actions and conduct of the parties. A contract exists when the parties agree on the sale, the price, and the particular animal. Large numbers of dogs and other animals are sold under an oral agreement.

When the buyer asks the seller what price he will take for a dog, to which the seller replies that he will take a certain sum, and the buyer says he will give it, the courts have said under such circumstances "it is difficult to conceive how, by acts or words, they could have given a better definition or more appropriate illustration of a contract of an immediate sale."

In either a written or oral contract to sell, the sale is consummated upon the payment of the consideration and the delivery of the animal. In Chapman v. Campbell, 13 Gratt. 109, the Virginia Supreme Court defined a consummated contract of sale of personal property as where there is a "contract for an immediate sale of a chattel and nothing remains to be done by the vendor, as between him and vendee, the vendor immediately acquires a property in the price and the vendee a property in the goods and then all the consequences resulting from the vesting of the property follows."

The delivery may be direct to the purchaser or to an agent designated by the purchaser. The seller may retain possession of the dog for a limited time even though title and ownership passes to the buyer. For example, when a professional handler owns a dog and he sells it to a person who then permits the handler to keep the dog for purposes of training or showing the dog. This is called symbolical or constructive delivery. Title passes, but actual possession remains with the seller under the terms and conditions agreed upon by the parties.

The sale of a purebred dog can be consummated and ownership can pass to the new owner without transferring or assigning the certificate of registration of the American Kennel Club. The requirements of the American Kennel Club for the registration of dogs do not affect the title to a dog as between the seller and the purchaser. The transfer of the certificate of registration is not necessary to consummate the sale of a dog registered with the American Kennel Club. But in order to register the offspring, there must be a compliance with their rules and requirements. The following are the American Kennel Club rules applying to registrations and listing of dogs.

Registration and Listing

SECTION 1. The breeder of a dog is the person who owned the dam of that dog when the dam was bred; except that if the dam was leased at the time of breeding, the breeder is the lessee.

SECTION 2. An American-bred dog is a dog whelped in the United States of America by reason of a mating which took place in the United States of America.

SECTION 3. Any person in good standing with The American Kennel Club may apply for the registration of any pure-bred or litter of pure-bred dogs owned by him, by supplying The American Kennel Club with such information and complying with such conditions as it shall require.

At present the fee for registration of each imported dog is two ($2.00) dollars, for each dog whelped in the United States of America, eighteen (18) months of age or under, two ($2.00) dollars, and for each dog whelped in the United States of America over eighteen (18) months of age, four ($4.00) dollars. Individual dogs under three months of age may be registered for one ($1.00) dollar each provided the litter registration application is accompanied by applications to register all the individual dogs of the litter.

SECTION 4. No individual dog from a litter whelped in the United States of America on or after January 1,

1932, shall be eligible for registration unless the litter has first been registered by the person who owned the dam at time of whelping; except that if the dam was leased at time of whelping, the litter must be registered by the lessee. A single dog of a registered litter shall be registered only by the owner of the dam at time of whelping, or by the next subsequent owner; except that if the dam is leased at time of whelping, the dog shall be registered only by the lessee of the dam at that time or by the next subsequent owner. No dog of such registered litter shall be eligible for entry in a dog show unless it is registered or listed as provided in this chapter.

At present the fee for litter registrations, the application for the registration of which shall be received within three months of the date of birth of the litter, is one ($1.00) dollar for each such litter, and for each litter the application for the registration of which shall be received after three months from the date of the birth of the litter the fee is two ($2.00) dollars.

SECTION 5. No dog or litter out of a dam under eight (8) months or over twelve (12) years of age at time of mating, or by a sire under seven (7) months or over twelve (12) years of age at time of mating, will be registered unless the application for registration shall be accompanied by an affidavit or evidence which shall prove the fact to the satisfaction of The American Kennel Club.

SECTION 6. No litter of pure-bred dogs and/or no single pure-bred dog which shall be determined by The American Kennel Club to be acceptable in all other respects for registration, shall be barred from registration because of the failure, by the legal owner of all or part of said litter, or said single dog to obtain some one or more of the signatures needed to complete the applicant's chain of title to the litter or dog sought to be registered, unless that person who, when requested, refuses to sign the application form shall furnish a reason therefore satisfactory to The American Kennel Club, such as the fact that at the time of service an agreement in writing was made between the owner or lessee of the sire and the owner or lessee of the dam to the effect that no application for registration should be made and/or that the produce of such union should not be registered. In all cases where such an agreement in writing has been made, any person disposing of any of the produce of such union must secure from the new owner a statement in writing that he receives such produce upon the understanding that it shall not be registered. For the purpose of registering or refusing to register pure-bred dogs The American Kennel Club will recognize only such conditional sale or conditional stud agreements affecting the registration of pure-bred dogs as are in writing and are shown to have been brought to the attention of the applicant for registration. The American Kennel Club cannot recognize alleged conditional sale, conditional stud or other agreements not in writing which affect the registration of pure-bred dogs, until after the existence, construction and/or effect of the same shall have been determined by an action at law.

The owner or owners of a stud dog pure-bred and eligible for registration who in print or otherwise asserts or assert it to be pure-bred and eligible for registration and on the strength of such assertion secures or permits its use at stud, must pay the cost of its registration. The owner or owners of a brood bitch pure-bred and eligible for registration who in print or otherwise asserts or assert it to be pure-bred and eligible for registration and on the strength of such assertion leases it or sells its produce or secures the use of a stud by promising a puppy or puppies as payment of the stud fee in lieu of cash, must pay the cost of its registration.

That person or those persons refusing without cause to sign the application form or forms necessary for the registration of a litter of pure-bred dogs or of a single pure-bred dog and that person or those persons refusing without cause to pay the necessary fees due from him, her or them to be paid in order to complete the chain of title to a pure-bred litter or a pure-bred single dog sought to be registered, when requested by The American Kennel Club, may be suspended from the privileges of The American Kennel Club or fined as the Board of Directors of The American Kennel Club may elect.

The registration of a single pure-bred dog out of a litter eligible for registration may be secured by its legal owner as a one-dog litter registration and the balance of the litter may be refused registration where the breeder or the owner or lessee of the dam at the date of whelping wrongfully has refused to register the litter and that person or those persons so wrongfully refusing shall be suspended from the privileges of The American Kennel Club or fined as the Board of Directors of The American Kennel Club may elect.

SECTION 7. No change in the name of a dog registered with The American Kennel Club will be allowed to be made.

SECTION 8. Registration of a dog with The American Kennel Club gives the dog the privilege of show competition for its life.

SECTION 9. If the owner of an apparently pure-bred dog shall be unable to supply all the information necessary for registration, and can and does furnish proof acceptable to The American Kennel Club that such dog is 'ineligible for registration' such dog may be listed with

The American Kennel Club for the purpose of being shown or exhibited at dog shows and may be shown for life without being registered upon payment of a listing fee on each occasion upon which it is entered.

A dog eligible for registration likewise can be listed with The American Kennel Club for the purpose of being shown or exhibited at dog shows but may only be shown at three separate events before application for registration is made. A listing fee must be paid on each occasion that the dog is shown without its registration number.

SECTION 10. In any case where the owner of a dog which is sought to be shown shall be delayed in securing the papers or information necessary for the registration of the dog, without fault on the part of such owner, or when application has been made to The American Kennel Club for registration of said dogs and defects which The American Kennel Club believes can be remedied have been found in the application for registration, written permission may be given by The American Kennel Club to show said dog for a reasonable time as a listed dog, if the owner shall so request, but a listing fee must be paid on each occasion upon which it is entered until the dog has been registered.

SECTION 11. If the name of a dog which has been listed with The American Kennel Club and which shall have won a prize at any dog show, subsequently shall be changed, the former name as well as the new name shall be given on the entry form for any subsequent shows and shall be published in the catalogs of such subsequent shows until such time as said dog shall have been awarded a prize in one of the regular official classes of The American Kennel Club under its new name whereupon its former name may be dropped.

SECTION 12. Any person in good standing with The American Kennel Club may apply for transfer of ownership to him of any registered dog acquired by him by supplying The American Kennel Club with such information and complying with such conditions as it shall require.

At present an application to record transfer of ownership of a registered dog which is received by the American Kennel Club within three months from the actual date when ownership was transferred, requires a fee of one dollar ($1.00); and an application received after three months from the actual date of transfer requires a fee of two dollars ($2.00).

Applications to record transfers which are received by the American Kennel Club attached to the original application to register a dog require a fee of one dollar ($1.00) for each transfer, in addition to the registration fee, regardless of the time elapsed between the actual date of transfer and the date the application is received.

SECTION 13. The American Kennel Club will not protect any person against the use by any other person of a kennel name in the registration of dogs with The American Kennel Club or in the entry of registered dogs in shows held under The American Kennel Club rules, unless the kennel name has been registered with The American Kennel Club.

SECTION 14. On and after October 1, 1948, applications for the use of a kennel name as a prefix in the registering and showing of dogs shall be made to The American Kennel Club on a form which will be supplied by said Club upon request, and said application must be accompanied by a fee, the amount of which shall be determined by The Board of Directors of The American Kennel Club. The Board will then consider such application and if it approves of the name selected will grant the right to the use of such name only as a prefix for a period of five (5) years.

At present the fee is fifteen ($15.00) dollars.

SECTION 15. The recorded owner shall have first consideration of the grant to use said kennel name for additional consecutive five (5) year terms upon receipt of the application for renewal accompanied by the renewal fee, the amount of which shall be determined by the Board of Directors, when received before the date of expiration of the original grant but the grant for any five (5) year renewal term will be made only at the expiration of the previous term.

At present the renewal fee is ten ($10.00) dollars.

In the event of the death of a recorded owner of a registered kennel name, his executors, administrators or legal heirs, upon submission of proper proof of their status may use the name as a prefix during the remainder of the five (5) year term of use and the legal heir of the deceased recorded owner, or the executors or administrators acting in his behalf, shall have first consideration of the grant to the use of said name for additional terms as provided heretofore in this section.

SECTION 16. If the recorded owner of a registered kennel name granted after October 1, 1948, desires to transfer ownership of or an interest in said kennel name to a new owner, application to transfer such name for the unexpired term must be made to The American Kennel Club on a form which will be supplied by said Club upon request. The application must be submitted for the approval of the Board of Directors of The American Kennel Club and accompanied by a fee, the amount of which shall be determined by the Board of Directors of The American Kennel Club.

Any kennel name granted by The American Kennel Club prior to October 1, 1948, may be transferred by its present owner or owners to another only by consent and on certain conditions and payment of fee as determined by the Board of Directors of The American Kennel Club.

At present the transfer fee is ten ($10.00) dollars.

SECTION 17. In the case of any registered kennel name which is recorded as jointly owned by two or more persons, application to transfer the interest of one co-owner to another co-owner, may be made to The American Kennel Club on a form which will be supplied by said Club upon request. The application must be submitted for the approval of the Board of Directors of the American Kennel Club but no fee will be charged for such a transfer.

SECTION 18. The protection of all kennel names registered between March 1, 1934, and October 1, 1948, shall depend upon their continuous use by registered owners. Neglect by the recorded owner of a registered kennel name to use such name in the registration of dogs for a continuous period of six years or more shall be considered such an abandonment of the name as to justify The American Kennel Club in refusing to protect its use unless the owner or owners thereof prior to the expiration of such six-year period shall notify the American Kennel Club of his, her or their desire to retain the same.

Warranty in the Sale of Dogs—General

In the sale of personal property, a warranty is an expressed or implied statement of the existence of a fact or a condition of the property which the seller guarantees as true. It is an agreement to be responsible for damages arising from false statements or assurance of a fact. For example, if the owner of a dog warrants that the dog is a pedigreed dog and registered with the American Kennel Club and a purchaser buys the dog relying upon these facts and later it is determined that the dog is a mongrel and is not registered with the American Kennel Club, the purchaser has the right to rescind the contract of sale and may sue for damages incurred. Warranties may be either expressed or implied.

Expressed Warranty

Expressed warranty can be either in writing or an oral statement. No particular form is required to constitute an expressed warranty. Any statement of condition, quality or fact about the animal during negotiations leading up to the sale which the purchaser relies upon in making up his mind to buy the animal is an expressed warranty.

A good example is the case of *McNeir vs. Greer-Hale Chinchilla Ranch*, 194 Va. 623, 74 SE (2) 165. McNeir purchased five pairs of chinchillas from Greer-Hale Chinchilla Ranch for $6,250.00. McNeir claimed that it was represented to him that each pair was composed of young, normal animals of breeding age and that they were normal reproducing-type chinchillas and not barren or impotent. He further alleged that he had relied upon those statements, but that the animals did not meet or measure up to the representations and warranty in that they were not young and normal, but were impotent or near-impotent, and did not produce a normal number of young. Greer admitted that McNeir told him he knew nothing about the business of breeding chinchillas, that he wanted Greer to select his stock, and that McNeir was buying the animals for breeding stock. Upon learning that the animals did not measure up to the seller's representations and warranty, McNeir offered to return them but his offer was declined.

The Court held:

The representations and statements that defendant

(McNeir) claimed were made by plaintiff (Greer) concerning the breeding qualities of the several pairs of chinchillas constituted a warranty of quality if, when the seller made them, he intended that they would be relied upon, and if they were in fact relied upon by defendant (McNeir) as an inducement to purchase.

The form in which representations of the vendor are made, and the words in which they are expressed, are, comparatively, unimportant. The true question is always the effect and intentions of the statements made by the vendor, and this (except when writings are to be construed) is a question for a jury.

It is important that the statements of the seller are expressed as facts distinguished from mere opinions or belief. The expression of an opinion with no intention of giving a guarantee or warranty is not binding. "I think this puppy will make a champion" is no warranty. It is merely an opinion or belief. But if the seller states: "This puppy is free of diseases and is a healthy puppy," it is a warranty. Should the puppy die of a disease it had at the time of the sale, the seller is liable for breach of the sale contract. The buyer may recover the amount paid for the puppy and reasonable expenses. But if the owner of a dog states orally or in writing that he warrants his dog to be sound in every way, free from disease and is a pedigreed dog eligible to be registered with the American Kennel Club, this is a guarantee to the buyer that if the dog is not as the seller has warranted the seller will be liable for breach of the sales contract and the buyer may rescind the contract, and recover the amount paid for the dog plus reasonable expenses.

Written warranties generally are not difficult to understand and leave very little for implications. The difficulty arises when there is an implied warranty.

Implied Warranty

An implied warranty is an understanding as to the conditions of the property to be sold that is assumed without being openly or directly expressed. It may be inferred from the circumstances of the sale.

It can be said that generally there is no implied warranty of competency or fitness in the sale of a dog where there is no fraud or misrepresentations. The maxim of *"Caveat Emptor,"* let the buyer beware, generally applies. For example, a young pup is purchased at a pet shop and nothing is said and the purchaser has had an opportunity to see and examine the pup; he purchases it at his own risk. The same rule applies when purchasing "show stock." If the buyer of the show stock examines the animals before entering into the contract of sale, for the purpose of satisfying himself as to their quality, he is estopped from claiming that there was any implied warranty as to the quality of the dogs for show purposes.

The above general rule of law has many exceptions. There are numerous situations where the rule of implied warranty applies. In the twenty-eight states where the new Commercial Code is in effect there is an implied warranty of fitness for a particular purpose for sale of all goods including animals. It provides that if the seller knows the particular purpose for which the goods are required, and the buyer relies on the seller's skill and judgment, there is, unless excluded, an implied warranty that the goods shall be fit for such purpose. For example, the purchase of a stud dog for breeding purposes would be a particular purpose, while the purchase of a dog for a pet would not be a particular purpose. The key is the term "fitness for a particular purpose."

In the states where the Commercial Code is not yet the law, the courts are holding that there is an implied warranty for fitness for a particular purpose.

An early case: where one sells another a jack to be used for the purposes of breeding mules, there is an implied warranty that the jack is reasonably suited to the use intended.

In the case of *Balch vs. Newberry*, 253 P. (2) 153, (1953) Okl., the evidence disclosed that the defendant seller was engaged in breeding and raising pedigreed dogs and had sold the plaintiff buyer a "stud" dog. In fact, he had sold the plaintiff other highly bred dogs. It was established that the seller knew that the dog was bought to be used exclusively for breeding purposes and the plaintiff relied upon the seller's judgment that the dog was of high breeding and fit for such purposes. Upon discovering the dog to be sterile, the buyer brought an action against the seller seeking to rescind the contract of sale. The court held that where a buyer trusts the judgment of the seller, who is engaged in the business of raising and selling stock to be used for breeding purposes, there is an implied warranty of its fitness. The buyer may rescind the contract for breach of implied warranty and recover what he paid under the contract and expenses necessarily incidental to the caring for the dog.

Where a dog is in the seller's possession, there is always an implied warranty that he owns the dog.

The law of the place where the sale was made and executed, although the parties may have resided elsewhere, governs as to whether warranties are to be implied or not.

4

Liability of the Owner for Acts of His Dog

Liability for Injuries by Dogs

There are two doctrines of law involved in determining the liability of an owner whose dog causes injuries: the common-law liability and the statutory liability. Some states adhere to the common-law doctrine and others have changed by statutes the liability of the owner or keeper of dogs. It is therefore most important in any case involving injuries caused by a dog to determine if the injuries occurred in a state controlled by the common-law liability or the statutory liability.

Common-Law Liability

At common law, the owner of a dog is not liable for injuries inflicted by his dog unless it is vicious and the owner knew or should have known this fact. But once it is shown that the dog is of a vicious character, and that the owner or person having possession of it has knowledge of such fact, the owner or keeper is liable for injuries caused by the dog. The reason for such doctrine is ex-

58

plained in an early case: the natural presumption from the habits of dogs is that they are tame, docile and harmless both as to persons and property and for that reason the owner or keeper is not liable for damages resulting from acts of the dog unless the owner or keeper has knowledge of the dog's vicious propensity. Therefore under the common-law liability the person injured by a dog must prove that the owner or keeper knew or should have known of the bad habits of his dog.

In most cases the courts talk about the "vicious propensity" of a dog. This term has been defined in the case of *Merritt vs. Matchett,* 135 Mo. 176, 115 S.W. 1066 as follows: "A vicious propensity is not confined to a disposition on the part of the dog to attack every person he might meet, but included as well, a natural fierceness or disposition to mischief as might occasionally lead him to attack human beings without provocation."

A good case for setting forth the common law doctrine of liability of a person who owns or keeps a dog is *Mungo vs. Bennett,* 119 SE(2) 522 (S.C.):

The authorities generally agree that all domestic animals, whether horses, mules, cattle, dogs, cats or others, are not presumed to be dangerous to persons, and before recovery of damages may be had against the owner the injured party must prove that the particular animal was of a dangerous, or vicious, nature and that this dangerous propensity was either known, or should have been known to the owner. The negligence that imposes liability upon the owner is the keeping of a dangerous animal with knowledge of its dangerous tendency, or in the failure to restrain it from injuring persons.

And, a vicious disposition " . . . is a propensity or tendency of an animal to do any act that might endanger the safety of the persons and property of others in a given situation. Although an animal is actuated solely by mischievousness or playfulness, rather than maliciousness or ferociousness, yet, if it has a tendency to do a dangerous or harmful act, it has a vicious propensity within the meaning of the rule holding the owner or keeper liable for injuries resulting from vicious propensities of which he has knowledge."

As to injuries by dogs, our Court applied these general principles in our early case of *M'Caskill v. Elliot*, 5 Strob. 196. This case exploded the popular notion that "a dog is entitled to one bite." It laid down what is now the well established general rule that if an owner has heard or seen enough "to put the owner on his guard and require him, as an ordinarily prudent man, to anticipate the injury that has occurred" (2 Am. Jur. 729), he has knowledge of the vicious or dangerous disposition. We quote therefrom:

"That a dog has once bitten a man, is a circumstance from which the probability of its biting another, may be inferred; but the same inference may be drawn with equal confidence from other indications of the dog's disposition. Indeed, attempts before made by a dog that had never succeeded in actually biting, may give more full assurance of danger to be apprehended from it, than could exist as to another dog, that under some peculiar circumstances had used its teeth upon man. To require that a plaintiff, before he can have redress for being bitten, should show that some other sufferer had previously endured harm from the same dog, would be always to leave the first wrong unredressed, and to lose sight of the thing to be proved in attention to one of the means of proof."

Under the common law where a dog roams abroad on another's land of its own accord and does damage or inflicts injury to persons, animals, or property, there can be no recovery therefor in the absence of a special statutory enactment, unless it be shown that (1) The dog was possessed of a propensity to commit the depredation complained of, and (2) The owner knew or was chargeable with knowledge of such propensity. This principle of law is grounded upon a recognition that by natural instinct and habit an ordinary dog of most breeds is inclined to roam around and stray at times from its immediate habitat without causing injury or doing damage to persons or property. And because of this natural instinct of dogs, the early common law did not require them to be kept shut up, but instead promulgated the foregoing rule which allows a reputable dog a modicum of liberty to follow his roaming instincts without imposing liability on its master.

The foregoing in brief is the applicable law. And it is interesting to observe that the liability thus imposed by these general principles upon owners of domestic animals instead of being relaxed, have been changed in some states by statute, " . . . so that the owner of a dog or other domestic animal may be liable for injuries inflicted by it, even though he did not know of its vicious or mischievous propensities."

Statutory Liability

Many states have changed the common-law theory of liability by enacting statutes governing the liability of the owner or keeper of a dog doing damage to person or property. The statutes are generally referred to as "Dog Bite Statutes." The Dog Bite Statutes vary in their terms from absolute liability to liability with many defenses. Generally speaking, however, such statutes which impose upon the owner or keeper of a dog liability for any damage done by the dog to person or property eliminates scienter as a necessary element of liability. That is, to recover, it is not necessary to prove that the owner or keeper knew or should have known that the dog had vicious habits.

Examples of states which have enacted Dog Bite statutes imposing liability on the dog owner without expressly authorizing any defense is California:

"The owner of any dog which bites any person while such person is on or in a public place or lawfully on or in a private place, including the property of the owner of such dog, shall be liable for such damages as may be suffered by the person bitten, regardless of such dog or owner's knowledge of such viciousness."

Connecticut statute states: " . . . when any dog shall do any damage either to body or property of any person the owner or keeper shall be liable for such damages."

Statute enacted in 1949 in the state of Florida authorizes certain defenses which the dog owner may be entitled to in an action for damages caused by his dog.

The owners of any dog which shall bite any person, while such person is on or in a public place, or lawfully on or in a private place, including the property of the owner of such dogs, shall be liable for such damages as may be suffered by persons bitten, regardless of the former viciousness of such dog or the owners' knowledge of such viciousness. A person is lawfully upon private property of such owner within the meaning of this Act when he is on such property in the performance of any duty imposed upon him by the laws of this state or by the laws or postal regulations of the United States, or when he is on such property upon invitation, expressed or implied, of the owner thereof: Provided, however, no owner of any dog shall be liable for any damages to any person or his property when such person shall mischievously or carelessly provoke or aggravate the dog inflicting such damage; nor shall any such owner be so liable if at the time of any such injury he had displayed in a prominent place on his premises a sign easily readable including the words "Bad Dog."

Statutes such as enacted in Wisconsin have been interpreted by the courts as not imposing absolute liability on the owner or keeper of a dog which caused injury to person or property. In the case of *Harris v. Hoyt,* 161 Wis. 498, 154 N.W. 842, the Court ruled: The statute providing that " . . . the owner or keeper of any dog which shall have injured or caused the injury of any person or property . . . shall be liable to the person so injured . . . for all damages so done, without providing notice to the owner or keeper of such dog or knowledge by him that his dog was mischievous" does not impose upon the owner or keeper an absolute liability to respond in damages to any one bitten no matter under what circumstances, but its purpose is merely to abrogate the necessity of belonging and providing scienter on the part of the owner or keeper.

A dog owner must consult the statutes of his particular state to determine his rights and liabilities for injuries caused by his dog. Dog owners and professional handlers who transport and show dogs in many states should remember that the law of the state where the dog causes damage will govern the liability and not the state where the owner or handler lives.

The following case holds that the dog bite statute is not limited to recovery for injuries resulting from the bite alone but imposes liability for any injury caused by the dog. *Gross v. Dunham,* 221 A(2) 555 (N. J. 1966).

"On May 4, 1963 the infant plaintiff was walking her dog on a public street in front of defendant's home, when the defendant's dog came running from the latter's premises and allegedly attacked her, knocked her to the ground, and then bit her leg."

The statute provides:

" 'The owner of any dog which shall bite a person while such person is on or in a public place, . . . shall be liable for such damages as may be suffered by the person bitten, regardless of the former viciousness of such dog or the owners' knowledge of such viciousness.' "

Plaintiffs allege that the statute is remedial in nature and should be accorded a liberal interpretation. They contend that a proper construction thereof grants the infant plaintiff the right to recover for her back injuries, without proof of scienter.

The Court said:

We have no case in this State which deals with this precise question. However, similar statutes have been given a liberal construction in other jurisdictions. California has such a statute. In *Hicks v. Sullivan,* 122 Cal. App. 635, 10 P.2d 516, 518 (D.Ct.App. 1932), where it was argued that liability of the dog owner was incurred only when the complainant was actually bitten, the court said:

"This statute does not purport to limit the recovery of damages actually suffered as the result of an attack by a savage dog, to the physical wound from biting."

In *Rossi v. Del Duca,* 344 Mass. 66, 181 N.E.2d 591 (Sup.Jud.Ct. 1962), the dog bite statute provided for recovery for "damage to either the body or property of any person." Defendant argued that such language must mean damage which is the direct result of injury to the person and could not include consequential damage sustained by the victim's father. The court disagreed, holding that the object of the statute was to protect from injury by dogs, and that such strict interpretation would fall short of giving complete redress for injuries by dogs.

We do not believe that N.J.S.A. 4:19–16 should receive the limited construction placed on it by the trial court and urged on appeal by defendant. The statute has been described as "distressingly ambiguous on its face." *Foy v. Dayko,* 82 N.J. Supra, 8, 13, 196 A 2d 535 (App. Div. 1964). We consider it to be remedial legislation entitled to a liberal interpretation.

Moreover, the "plain meaning" of the statute . . . is not limited to recovery for injuries resulting from the bite alone. It imposes liability *for such damages as may be suffered by the person bitten.* For example, if a person is bitten by a vicious dog and during the same incident receives an eye laceration caused by the dog's paw, we consider the damage for the eye injury to be "damages . . . suffered by the person bitten," as contemplated by the statute.

We conclude that a person who is bitten by a dog and suffers other injuries during the attack is entitled to recover from the dog owner for all of the injuries sustained. The statute is entitled to a reasonable construction.

Defenses the Owner or Keeper May Rely Upon

As indicated in the *Mungo* case, the common-law theory of liability is that the person injured must prove that the dog was vicious and that the owner knew or should have known the character of his dog. Therefore, in addition to the defenses that the owner is entitled to under the statutory theory of liability, which will be discussed below, the owner or keeper under the common-law doctrine is entitled to the defense that he did not have knowledge of the vicious propensities of his dog. In actions for damages such as injuries caused by a dog, the question of whether the owner had knowledge of the use of ordinary care or should have known of the dog's vicious propensities is a question for the jury to determine.

Some of the important defenses the owner may rely upon in defending an action for damages caused by a dog under dog bite statutes and common-law doctrine are as follows:

1. The dog did not commit the act.

2. The person seeking to recover damages intentionally provoked the dog into committing the act that caused the injury.

3. Contributory negligence on the part of the person claiming damages.

4. The person alleging damages assumed the risk of being injured.

The first defense listed above needs no explanation since the owner merely relies upon the fact that his dog did not cause the damages claimed. Where the evidence is conflicting it is for the jury to determine if the person claiming damages is entitled to recover from all the facts.

The other three defenses can best be illustrated by cases involving the different theories. In the case of *Vandercar vs. David*, 96 So. (2) 227, decided by the Supreme Court of Florida in 1957, the plaintiff brought an action for damages against the defendant, the dog owner, for injuries she alleged she sustained when the dog caused her to fall. The owner claimed she was guilty of contributory negligence and assumption of risk by playing with and exciting the dog so as to provoke the dog's playful conduct which caused the fall.

The case went to the jury on the issue whether the defendant's dog caused the plaintiff's fall. The evidence on that issue included some facts of a kind which could have been relied on to establish assumption of risk by the plaintiff, through inciting and provoking or inducing the dog's playful conduct which caused her to fall.

The question here, then, is whether the defenses of contributory negligence or assumption of risk are available to a dog owner who is sued for injury to a person caused by his dog, other than by biting.

The rule established by the authorities is that while liability of an owner of a dog is based on an obligation as insurer rather than on negligence, and contributory negligence as such is not a defense nevertheless, if an injured party unnecessarily and voluntarily puts himself in the way to be hurt, knowing the probable consequences, he may be deemed to have assumed the risk and to have induced his injury.

In *Wojewoda v. Rybarczyk*, 246 Mich 641, 225 NW 555, speaking of a statute imposing liability on dog owners for injuries caused by their dogs, the Michigan Court said:

"This statute eliminates the necessity which existed at common law of averring and proving that the dog had vicious propensities . . . , and the owner's knowledge thereof . . .

"The basis of liability is not negligence in the manner of keeping and confining the animal but in keeping him at all. The owner is liable under this statute, even though the dog is taken out of his inclosure [sic] by his servants in disobedience of his orders . . .

"It is, however, a defense if the injured party voluntarily brought on the injury himself, with the full knowledge of its probable consequences."

Smythe v Schacht, 93 Cal App 2d 315, 209 P2d 114, 117, involved a statute which imposed liability on the dog owner without expressly authorizing any defense, and which was worded as follows:

"The owner of any dog which shall bite any person while such person is on or in a public place, or lawfully on or in a private place, including the property of the owner of such dog, shall be liable for such damages as may be suffered by the person bitten, regardless of the former viciousness of such dog or the owner's knowledge of such viciousness . . . ."

Under the particular facts of that case it was held that the defense of assumption of risk was not established, but the Court recognized the right to assert the defense, and said:

" . . . We entertain no doubt that in adopting the statute here in question the legislature did not intend to make the liability of the owner absolute and render inoperative certain principles of law such as assumption of risk or wilfully inviting injury, which over a long period of time have been established in our system of jurisprudence. While the Dog Bite Statute does not found the liability on negligence, good morals and sound reasoning dictate that if a person lawfully upon the portion of another's property where the biting occurred should kick, tease, or otherwise provoke the dog, the law should and would recognize the defense that the injured person by his conduct invited injury and therefore, assumed the risk thereof.

"In Vol. 3, Corpus Juris Secundum, Animals, §150, page 1254, it is said: 'Contributory negligence will defeat recovery in an action for injuries caused by a domestic animal where negligence is the gist of the action; but, where it is not, more than ordinary contributory negligence is necessary to relieve the defendant from liability.'

"And on page 1255 of 3 C.J.S., §150, we find the following: 'It must be established that the injury is at-
tributable not to the keeping of the animal but to the
injured party's voluntary act in putting himself in a way
to be hurt, knowing the probable consequences thereof
so that he may fairly be deemed to have brought the
injury on himself; but if this is shown recovery will be
defeated.'"

This principle that a person can not make his own
negligent or wrongful act the ground for recovering
damages from another has received general recognition and application in cases of this kind.

As can be seen from the above cases, contributory negligence is a good defense both under the common-law
doctrine and the statutory doctrine. This principle is followed by the majority of jurisdictions which have considered the question.

Some jurisdictions not allowing the defense of contributory negligence to be used follow the rule that if a person
with knowledge of the evil disposition of a dog voluntarily
and unnecessarily places himself in the way of the dog
he cannot recover from the owner or keeper of the dog
for injuries resulting from the actions of the dog. The
leading case is *Muller v. McKesson*, 73 N.Y. 195, which
enunciated this rule.

A night watchman employed by the defendants sustained injuries when he entered the gate to the factory
owned by the defendants. He was bitten by a Siberian
bloodhound belonging to the defendants. The defendants
set up the defense of contributory negligence, assumption
of risk, and the negligence of a fellow servant rule. The
dog was allowed to run loose in the factory yard at night
but was tied up during the day. He was informed by the

engineer when the dog was loose. The morning of the accident the engineer did not inform him that the dog was loose. As the night watchman entered the factory he was bitten. The Court said that in order for the owner or keeper of a dog to defend on the grounds of contributory negligence the owner or keeper must prove acts which would establish that the person injured voluntarily brought the calamity upon himself or that he wantonly excited the dog or that he voluntarily and unnecessarily put himself in the way of the dog knowing of the dog's evil propensities. The trial court held that the night watchman was entitled to recover as a matter of law and the Appellate Court affirmed the lower court.

In many states the Courts have held that a person injured by a dog as a result of his intentionally provoking the dog is barred from recovering damages from the owner or keeper of the dog.

In the case of *Kightlinger* vs. *Egan*, 65 Ill. 235 the Court held that plaintiff could not recover for a dog bite, because he had kicked the dog, and could therefore not claim that the dog was dangerous or savage. The court said, "the plaintiff should not be allowed to recover for damages caused by his own wrong."

In *Worthen* vs. *Love*, 60 Vt. 285, 14 A 461, the plaintiff went to the barn where the owner kept a vicious dog chained and provoked the dog to break the chain, thus injuring the plaintiff. The court reasoned that the plaintiff was not entitled to recover because he had committed an unlawful act in provoking the dog and had had no lawful reason to go to the barn where the dog was chained.

There was a different ruling by the New York Court in *Schilling* vs. *Smith*, 78 N.Y.S. 586, where a twelve-year-

old boy who was mentally retarded teased and provoked
a vicious dog over a period of months. The evidence disclosed that the boy did not realize the teasing and provoking of the dog might cause the dog to bite him. The court
held that the boy could recover for injuries sustained as a
result of the bite of the dog. The boy was not mentally
capable of contributory negligence.

Courts in California, Connecticut, Georgia, Illinois,
Maine, Ohio, Rhode Island and Wisconsin have considered the question of intentional provocation of a dog by
a person who was injured and have held that the person
injured will be barred from recovering. To recover one
should come into court "without fault." The principle of
law is that when a person's conduct toward a dog or other
animal is knowingly such as is calculated to incite or provoke it to acts of damage, its naturally resulting action in
so far as it involves consequences to the inciter or pro-
voker is to be regarded in law as his and referable to him
and not to the animal.

Whether a person is guilty of intentionally provoking
a dog is one of fact which generally must be decided by a
jury from all the evidence of the case. The following cases
will illustrate the holding of courts in different jurisdictions.

One of the early leading cases is *Muller* vs. *McKesson,*
73 N.Y. 195, which laid down the rule of contributory
negligence followed by many courts. The court said that
to enable an owner or keeper of a dog to defend on the
ground of want of care acts should be proved which would
establish that the person injured voluntarily brought the
calamity upon himself. And if the person with full knowledge of the evil propensities of an animal wantonly excites

him or voluntarily and unnecessarily puts himself in the way of such an animal he ought not to be entitled to recover.

A Kentucky Court in *Burke* vs. *Fischer* 298 Ky. 157, 182 S.E.(2) 638 (1944) said that if a person having knowledge of the vicious propensities of a dog "wantonly excites him or voluntarily and unnecessarily places himself in position to be attacked, he will be held to have brought on the injury and ought not to be entitled to recover."

In *Brown* vs. *Barber* 26 Tenn. App.534, 174 S.W.(2) 298 (1943), the plaintiff ignored a sign reading "Keep Out, Bad Dog." The plaintiff entered an automobile service station by the rear door after closing time to get his car. The dog was fastened by a 6-foot chain. The dog barked as the plaintiff approached and an employee warned the plaintiff not to go around the dog. The plaintiff ignored the warning and walked up to the dog. The dog bit him. The trial court dismissed the action and the judgment was affirmed on appeal. The court held that the plaintiff could not recover for the reason that he was guilty of reckless indifference to the consequences and that he fully appreciated the danger and voluntarily incurred the risk of the very injury he sustained.

Normally trespassers cannot recover but the following cases decided in 1962, 1964 and 1965 will indicate the exception—especially involving children.

Rossi vs. Del Duca, 181 N.E.(2) 591 (Mass. 1962), the plaintiff, "Patricia Rossi, a minor, who seeks by her next friend to recover for injuries inflicted upon her by two dogs owned by the defendant, Ernest V. Del Duca."

In September, 1955, Ida Celia and the plaintiff, both aged eight, were students in the third grade of the Ashford school. In the afternoon of September 26, school having closed, they started walking up Oak Street toward their homes. As they reached the corner of Cambridge Street, they saw the German Weimaraner ahead of them on Oak Street. The dog started to come toward them, and, as the plaintiff testified, "We got frightened so we . . . ran down Cambridge Street . . . [and the dog was] following us." Realizing that Cambridge Street was a dead-end street, the girls left Cambridge Street on the north side passing around the garage at 70 Cambridge Street and the shed. The dog continued to follow them. After they passed the shed, they ran along a path in the field belonging to the defendant's father. The plaintiff then saw, for the first time, a black great Dane. "[T]he dog was on its hind legs and it was going to jump on her. It did jump on her. She didn't feel anything but they were biting her neck. She shouted for help." The plaintiff's father observed the defendant's great Dane dogs in the field. They "were worrying some object" which he learned was his daughter Patricia who was "crouched down on her knees . . . with her hands on her face." He picked her up and took her to the hospital.

The defendant testified that on September 26, 1955, he owned two "black Dane dogs." The dogs were "trained to stay in the field to the rear of this defendant's home where his equipment was kept. . . . He had a lot of equipment and was concerned about it." The defendant's arrangement with his father regarding this land was that the "defendant could use all of that property for parking his equipment and doing anything he wanted with it in connection with his business. . . . He had full control of the field."

[1,2] 1. It is clear both from the pleadings and the evidence that the plaintiff seeks to recover under G.L. c. 140, §155, which, as amended by St.1934, c. 320, §18

reads: "If any dog shall do any damage to either the body or property of any person, the owner or keeper, or if the owner or keeper be a minor, the parent or guardian of such minor, shall be liable for such damage, unless such damage shall have been occasioned to the body or property of a person who, at the time such damage was sustained, was committing a trespass or other tort, or was teasing, tormenting or abusing such dog." Under this statute, unlike the common law, "the owner or keeper of a dog is liable . . . for injury resulting from an act of the dog without proof . . . that its owner or keeper was negligent or otherwise at fault, or knew, or had reason to know, that the dog had any extraordinary, dangerous propensity, and even without proof that the dog in fact had any such propensity." *Leone v. Falco*, 292 Mass. 299, 300, 198 N.E. 273, 274. It is to be noted that the strict liability imposed by the statute is of no avail to a plaintiff if at the time of his injury he "was committing a trespass or other tort, or was teasing, tormenting or abusing such dog." And it is incumbent upon a plaintiff to plead and prove that he has done none of these things. *Sullivan v. Ward*, 304 Mass. 614, 24 N.E. 2d 672, 130 A.L.R. 437.

[3,4] The defendant contends that the plaintiff is barred from recovery because on her own testimony—and there is no evidence more favorable to her—she was committing a trespass at the time the defendant's dogs attacked her. We assume that, although the field where the plaintiff was attacked was owned by the defendant's father, the defendant had possessive rights in the property sufficient to render the principle enunciated in *Sarna v. American Bosch Magneto Corp.*, 290 Mass. 340, 195 N.E. 328, inapplicable. See *Moore v. Worcester Insulation Co.*, Inc., 338 Mass. 44, 153 N.E. 2d 646. We are of opinion, nevertheless, that the jury could have found that the plaintiff was not a trespasser, as that

word is used in the statute. A finding was warranted that the plaintiff, an eight year old girl, was frightened by the German Weimaraner dog which was between her and the only means of access to her house; that she turned and ran down a side street; and that because this was a dead-end street she went north across the field in the rear of the defendant's house in order to get home, the Weimaraner following her all the while. This evidence brings the case, we think, within the principle that one is privileged to enter land in the possession of another if it is, or reasonably appears to be, necessary to prevent serious harm to the actor or his property.

We assume that the statute evidences a legislative recognition of the right of a possessor of land to keep a dog for protection against trespassers. Nevertheless, we do not believe that the Legislature intended to bar recovery in a case like the present.

Messa vs. *Sullivan Key Club*, 209 N.E. (2) 872 (Illinois 1965).

Betty Messa brought this action against James Sullivan, Helen Sullivan and the Keyman's Club, an Illinois not for profit corporation, to recover damages for the bodily injuries which she sustained as the result of being bitten by the defendants' dog. The complaint was based on two theories: first, a common law action for the keeping of a vicious animal and, second, an action based on what is commonly known as the "Dog Bite Statute."

The plaintiff suffered her injuries in the Keyman's Club building, 4721 West Madison Street in the City of Chicago. . . . In addition, the apartment contained the defendants' furniture, personal property and their three year old German Shepherd dog, named "K.C.," which was kept there to protect the Club's property in the apartment. The various businesses located in the building were advertised by signs on the exterior of the structure and on a building directory which was located in the building lobby. There were, however, no notices anywhere that the fifth floor was used as a residence and not for commercial or business purposes.

The plaintiff, who was a deaf mute, testified that at about two o'clock on the afternoon of June 12, 1961, she entered the defendants' building for the purpose of selling printed cards depicting the deaf and dumb alphabet. She said that this was the first time she had been in the building; that as she walked through the lobby she saw a woman at a telephone switchboard in the building office, that she entered the elevator and rode it to the fifth floor. When she got to that floor, the door on the elevator itself opened automatically. The plaintiff said that before she could step out of the elevator she had to manually open a second door which swung outward. She opened this door, which she said was heavy. She stepped out into the fifth floor hall and turned to the left where there was a door. At this point the defendants' dog ran out of the door and jumped on the plaintiff. She testified: " . . . the dog bit me on the leg, and he bit me on the body, and he bit me on the arm, and I tried to cover my face. And the dog was big, and the dog was bigger than I was, and he was on top of me, and three times he bit me." The plaintiff stated that she finally managed to get back to the elevator and to ride down to the lobby where she told the woman at the switchboard what had happened.

During her testimony, the plaintiff was shown plaintiff's exhibit number one, a picture of a sign reading in large letters:

WARNING
KEEP OUT
VICIOUS
POLICE DOGS
INSIDE

She identified the exhibit as a picture of a sign which was posted on the manually operated elevator door which swung outward into the fifth floor hall. However, she denied having seen the sign because, in her words, ". . . the door was so heavy. I was pushing the door, it was a sliding door, and I did not see the sign."

Concerning her injuries, the plaintiff identified two exhibits as accurate pictures of the large marks and wounds inflicted by the dog on her leg, on her right side and on her right arm. The plaintiff testified that the bites left "holes" in her arm, that she felt pain for about two months after the occurrence and that she could not sleep for two weeks after the events in question.

The "Dog Bite Statute" with which this appeal is principally concerned provides:

"If a dog, without provocation, attacks or injures any person who is peaceably conducting himself in any place where he may lawfully be, the owner of the dog is liable in damages to the person so attacked or injured to the full amount of the injury sustained. The term 'owner' includes any person harboring or keeping a dog. The term 'dog' includes both male and female of the canine species."

This court, in *Beckert v. Risberg*, 50 Ill. App. 2d 100, 199 N.E. 2d 811, set forth the four elements of an action under this statute as follows:

(1) injury caused by a dog owned or harbored by the defendant;
(2) lack of provocation;
(3) peaceable conduct of the person injured, and
(4) the presence of the person injured in a place where he has a legal right to be.

. . . The defendants contend that the other elements are not satisfied, however, because the plaintiff's entry onto the fifth floor past a large sign warning her of the presence of the dog which bit her constituted an unlawful entry by the plaintiff and constituted provocative behavior on her part.

[1] We do not agree that the plaintiff was not lawfully on the defendants' premises. . . . Persons entering the building and riding its elevator would have no reason to believe that the fifth floor was used for residential purposes or that vicious dogs were kept there. The sole warning to this effect was posted in a place where it could be seen only split seconds before one would enter the danger area and only at a time when the elevator passenger would be concerned with pushing open the heavy door in order to step into the hall and continue on with his business there. We agree with the trial court that under these circumstances the warning sign was in the wrong location, that it did not give adequate warning of the danger and that hence the sign gives no grounds for holding that persons who enter the hall have no legal right to be there.

The cases primarily relied on by the defendants are distinguishable on their facts and are not applicable here. In *Fullerton v. Conan*, 87 Cal.App.2D 354, 197 P.2d 59, the California District Court of Appeal affirmed a judgment for the defendant in a case brought by a five year old child to recover for injuries she received when bitten by the defendant's dog. She had sued under the California "Dog Bite Statute" which, like our own statute, required that the plaintiff lawfully be on the dog owner's premises. In that case, however, unlike the present case, it appears that the child had been given a direct, oral instruction not to go into the yard where the dog was. In another California dog bite case, *Gomes v. Byrne*, 51 Cal. 2d 418, 333 P.2d 754, the court affirmed a judgment for the defendant. That case is not like the case at bar because there the plaintiff saw and heard the dog before he entered the yard where the dog was kept.

Warner vs. *Wolfe* 199 N.E. (2) 860 (Ohio 1964)

The plaintiff, a minor eight years of age, by and through his father filed a petition for damages sustained as a result of injuries alleged to have been received while he was on the premises of the defendant when he was severely bitten by three large dogs owned by the defendant.

Plaintiff alleges that the defendant owned and harbored the animals for the sole and only purpose of injuring the plaintiff and others who might enter upon such premises, that such animals were vicious and ferocious dogs, and that defendant knew or should have known that they were vicious and ferocious.

The premises of the defendant was a junkyard enclosed by a fence. Plaintiff alleges that there was in front of the premises a hinged gate or door for access to the premises, and that he and another boy entered the premises by means of a board which they found leaning against the outside of such gate or entranceway.

The defendant, in his answer, admits ownership of the dogs, alleges that the gates were secured by chain and lock at the time mentioned in plaintiff's petition, denies that the dogs were vicious or ferocious or kept in a negligent manner, alleges that the plaintiff was a trespasser upon the premises, and denies liability.

The case was tried to a jury, and the jury found, in answer to interrogatories, that the three dogs owned and harbored by the defendant were vicious, that the defendant knew or should have known that they were vicious, *that the defendant was negligent in harboring the dogs,* and that the negligence consisted of a failure to post signs warning of the presence of the dogs and to repair the defective gate, and awarded a verdict in favor of the plaintiff in the sum of $6,350.

The controlling question in this appeal is: Does Section 955.28, Revised Code, abrogate the common law of Ohio with respect to liability of dog owners or harborers for damage or injury caused by a vicious dog?

Section 955.28, Revised Code, provides as follows:

"*A dog that chases, worries, injures, or kills a person, sheep, lamb, goat, kid, domestic fowl, or domestic animal except a cat or another dog can be killed at any time or place. If, in attempting to kill such dog running at large, a person wounds it, he is not liable to prosecution under the penal laws which punish cruelty to animals. The owner or keeper shall be liable for any damage or injuries caused by a dog unless such damage or injury was to the body or property of a person who, at the time such damage or injuries were sustained, was committing a trespass on the property of the owner, or was teasing, tormenting or abusing such dog on the owner's property.*"

"In the case of *Lisk, Adm'r. v. Hora* (1924), 109 Ohio St. 519, 143 N.E. 545, the first paragraph of the syllabus sets forth the law with regard to the question here presented, as follows:

"The right to maintain an action at common law for damages resulting from injuries, which by his negligence the owner of a dog suffers such animal to commit, has not been abrogated by statute and such suit may be maintained either under the statute or at common law."

This rule is also set forth in 3 C.J.S. p. 1257, Animals 2. Injuries by Dogs, §151b Statutory Liability (1) In General, as follows:

"The common-law rule of liability may be altered or extended by statutes imposing an absolute duty upon the owner or keeper of dogs. . . . Although such statutes operate to create a new and different cause of action in no way dependent upon common-law principles, ordinarily they are not regarded as abrogating the common-law right of action for injuries caused by dogs, and suit may be maintained either under the statutes or at common-law . . . " Citing *Lisk v. Hora*, supra.

"With reference to the common-law action, 3 C.J.S. p. 1256, §151, states:

"Gist of action. Although it is said that at common law the liability is based on negligence, the gist of the action for injury by a dog known by its owner to be vicious is generally said to be not negligence in the manner of keeping the dog, but for keeping it at all. . . . The negligence on which liability is founded is keeping the animal with knowledge of its propensities."

See 4 American Jurisprudence (2d), 353, Animals, Section 105, Trespassers, where it is stated:

"The authorities almost unanimously hold that the owner of a domestic animal, known by him to be vicious and disposed to attack people, is bound to restrain it even as against a trespasser on his own premises, and that he will not be permitted to set up the commission of the trespass as a defense."

The reasoning upon which this rule is founded is similar to the reasoning of this court with regard to the spring-gun, trap or dangerous-instrument cases,

[1] Section 955.28, Revised Code, recreates a statutory action which had been established previously in Section 5838, General Code, which imposed a rule of absolute liability upon the owner or harborer of a dog for injury done to a person under certain conditions. This section does not abrogate the action which exists under the common law for damage or injuries inflicted upon property or a person by a vicious dog against a person who owns or harbors such a vicious dog, when he knows or should know those propensities of the dog.

[2] In this case, the jury found that the three dogs owned and harbored by the defendant were vicious, that the defendant knew or should have known that

they were vicious, and that the defendant was negligent in harboring the dogs. These findings constitute the gist of the common-law action for harboring vicious dogs.

Intentional and willful actions of the owner or keeper in setting his dog upon another cannot rely upon the defense of contributory negligence or the assumption of risk. Even a trespasser can recover when the owner of a dog willfully and intentionally causes the dog to attack and injury results.

In the case of *Zink* vs. *Foss*, 108 N.E. 906 (Mass. 1915) a young boy bitten by a dog sued for damages, claiming that the owner intentionally and willfully caused the dog to bite the youngster while the boy was trespassing on the lands belonging to the owner of the dog. The owner of the dog set up the defense that the boy was not entitled to recover because he was a trespasser. The court ruled that a trespasser can recover for injuries inflicted upon him by the active, willful and reckless misconduct of the owner.

Owner's Obligation to Handler or Owner of a Boarding Kennel

The owner of a dog who places the dog in the care of a handler or in a boarding kennel and fails to inform the handler or kennel-owner that the dog is vicious is liable should the dog cause injury. In a recent case the owner of a dog placed the dog in a boarding kennel while he went on vacation. The dog bit two persons causing considerable damage. The owner had not disclosed to the kennel owner the vicious nature of the dog. The owner of the boarding kennel was attacked by the dog and severely injured. The Court held the owner guilty of negligence in failing to disclose to the keeper of the dog's vicious nature. In this case the owner was well aware of his dog's prior tendencies to bite and it became his duty to so inform any person with whom he entrusted the dog.

Liability of Owner When His Dog Injures or Kills Another Dog

The owner of a dog injured or killed by another dog may recover damages under certain circumstances. A good case in point to illustrate the law is *Kling v. U. S. Fire Insurance Co.*, 146 So. (2) 635.

The owner of an unregistered female Terrier brought an action to recover damage for the death of the dog caused by the defendant's Boxer. The parties lived in the same neighborhood. The Terrier weighed nine pounds and the Boxer seventy-five pounds. Both dogs ran loose in the neighborhood. The Boxer attacked the Terrier and injured her so seriously that she died shortly after being taken to the veterinarian. The owner of the Terrier charged the owner of the Boxer with knowingly harboring a vicious and a dangerous animal. Substantiating the allegation the Terrier owner proved that the Boxer had bitten a child, killed a cat and injured two other dogs. The owner of the Boxer denied the allegations of harboring a vicious and dangerous animal and claimed the Terrier owner assumed the risk and was contributory negligent in permitting his small dog to run at large when large dogs might injure or kill her.

There were two questions before the Court. Was the Boxer a vicious and dangerous animal?

The court found that the Boxer had such qualities, as

evidenced by his attack on the Terrier. The four prior attacks supported this finding.

The second question: had the Boxer acted in such a fashion as to indicate these tendencies to his owner prior to the time he attacked the Terrier? The Court held that the modern and more reasonable doctrine is that an owner need not have had actual notice to make him chargeable: notice that the disposition of the animal was such that it would be likely to commit an injury similar to the one complained of is sufficient.

Before the owner of a dog can be held liable for injuring or killing another dog, it must be proven that his dog is savage or dangerous and that the owner knew or should have known that his dog bore dangerous propensities. The courts have gone so far as to say even if the dog has the habit of biting in play and the owner knew or should have known of such habits, he is liable. In an Illinois case the owner was held chargeable for injuries inflicted by a mule upon a servant; although the owner acted without actual knowledge of the animal's vicious disposition, the facts were deemed sufficient to prove that the master, by the exercise of diligence, would have known of such tendency. Knowledge, therefore, may be implied from circumstances.

Thus, in cases involving the conduct of animals causing injury to person or property of another, the inquiry is whether the owner actually knew the animal's malicious inclination; or, if he did not, whether its acts of viciousness were of such notoriety or frequency and with such nearness or in such circumstances as to cause a reasonable man, exercising due care over his own property for the protection of the rights of others, to take notice of the evil propensity. If he did not know—and had no reasonable grounds to suspect—the existence of any tendency to malevolence or viciousness on the part of his animal and was not cognizant of any acts of violence or depredation committed by it—or, if committed, the acts were done under circumstances of which he was wholly unaware or of which he would not have known if he had been ordinarily diligent and prudent in the management and control of the animal—he is not liable in damages; otherwise he is so liable.

Landlord and Tenant Relationship

The landlord owns his property and has the right to limit the use of his premises in any manner he so desires. The tenant has the privilege to agree to the terms of the landlord or refuse to enter into a rental agreement. If the landlord refuses to permit pets in the building and the tenant has knowledge of the landlord's policy, the courts will enjoin a tenant who attempts to keep a pet on the premises. If the lease states "no pets" or if the lease states "pets allowed" there is no problem as to the rights of the landlord and the tenant.

But there are exceptions to the general rule, as in the case where the tenant kept a dog in his apartment without first obtaining his landlord's written consent as required by the lease. More than three years after the dog had been obtained by the tenant, the landlord made objections and sued to recover the possession of the apartment on grounds the tenant had breached the lease. The landlord had known of the dog for two years. The court held the landlord impliedly gave consent to the keeping of the dog and thereby waived the provision of the lease.

The landlord must act promptly when a tenant violates the terms or he may waive his rights under the terms of the lease. As one court held: "Even where the prohibition is absolute it has been held that long inaction on the part of the landlord under circumstances implying knowledge on his part, may constitute a waiver of the prohibition itself."

Difficulty occurs when the lease is silent of any statement regarding pets and there is no general policy known to the tenant at the time of the executing of the lease. It can be said that ordinarily, where the lease is silent on the subject the tenant has the implied right to use the premises as he pleases, which includes keeping of a dog. However, in apartment houses, custom and policy may be a determining factor. If pets have never been kept and the lease is silent, the law would imply an obligation on the part of the tenant not to keep a dog.

A landlord may conditionally grant tenants permission to keep a dog, subject to the withdrawal if other tenants object. If the other tenants object and the landlord withdraws the permission, the courts will uphold the landlord and grant possession of the premises to the landlord on the grounds that the tenant has breached the lease agreement by not removing the dog.

It is important for an owner of a dog to provide in the lease for permission to keep a dog in order to be safe.

Even where the landlord permits the keeping of a dog by the tenant, the manner in which the dog or dogs are kept by the tenant may cause eviction. An Ohio court held that where a tenant kept several dogs in an apartment it constituted a nuisance. The Judge said, "Dogs do have their place and this court is in no way condemning the dog as a pet. The fault here is not the dog as a pet, it was the manner in which they were kept."

The law of the place where the rented property is located governs the rights of the parties in relationship to landlord and tenant.

Liability of a Motorist for Injuring or Killing Dogs On the Highway

Because of the more enlightened modern conceptions of the nature of dogs as domestic animals and their value and status as property, the courts are recognizing that there is a right of action against one who negligently kills or injures a dog. This is especially true where the owner has licensed the dog and is paying taxes. Dogs are valuable, are subject to taxation, and stealing them is put on a par with the larceny of any other personal property. There is no good reason why this substantial property right should not be accorded the same protection as other species of property.

In general a motorist can be held liable for injuring or killing a dog upon a highway if he is negligent in operating his motor vehicle. The person claiming the loss must prove that the driver was negligent: Examples of negligence include operating a motor vehicle at a speed that is greater than was reasonable and safe, having due regard for the conditions then existing; operating a motor vehicle without exercising due caution with respect to dogs that might be in, on or upon the highway; operating a motor vehicle without efficient and serviceable brakes; operating a motor vehicle with defective front headlights; failing to keep a motor vehicle under proper control so as to avoid endangering the property of persons or animals that might be in or upon a public highway; and failing to keep a proper lookout. There are many acts and omissions of negligence, depending upon the facts and circumstances of each case.

While a motorist is required to exercise reasonable care to avoid a collision with animals on a highway, he is not an insurer against injury. If the injury occurs which is unavoidable he is not liable.

In the case of *Flowerree vs. Thornbury,* 183 SW 359 (1916) the owner sued for damages for the killing of his Foxhound. The driver of the automobile ran over the dog, which was running loose on the highway. There was no evidence the driver was reckless or negligent. There was evidence that the Foxhound miscalculated, while attempting to cross the road in front of the car. The court held that the driver of the motor vehicle had the right to assume that the dog would exercise the ordinary instincts of such an animal and would keep out of the way of the automobile. The driver was not bound to look out for its safety unless he discovered the dog in time to have avoided striking it by such care as an ordinarily prudent person would exercise under the same circumstances.

Weathers vs. Friedland, 155 A 18 (1931): the owner sued for loss of a dog killed by the driver of a motor vehicle. The owner of the dog was returning from an evening walk, during which he had the dog on a leash. Upon arriving near his home he turned his dog loose; whereupon it darted into the roadway and was run over and killed. The driver of the car was driving on the left side of the road preparatory to turn into his driveway, some 75 feet away. The car had what was described as "cow lights." The court said:

We are unable to find negligence on the part of the driver of the car. It is said he was on the wrong side of the road. But whether the left side is the wrong side must naturally depend upon circumstances. We assume that the dog was not so highly trained as to be governed in its direction by the same regulations that controlled the reciprocal movements of traffic. Conditions permitting, the driver had the right to make such use of the roadway as was necessary to enable him to circle into his driveway. He could scarcely be expected to anticipate that, without warning, a dog would leap from the curb through the darkness into his path. The fact that the plaintiff (owner of the dog) had kept the dog in leash until that particular spot had been reached gives rise to the presumption that the animal was expected when released to do precisely what it did do, namely, bound homeward across the street. The plaintiff was responsible for that movement, and it was that that caused the mishap. We think that if there was negligence at all, it was on the part of the plaintiff; and that such negligence was contributory to, if not directly responsible for, the injury.

In the case of *Baker vs. Koplan*, 63 A (2) 279, decided in 1949, a hunting dog was tied by a chain to a doghouse 15 feet from the driveway going to the barn. The dog chain was 15 to 24 feet in length. The driver of a dual-wheel truck came to the farm for the purpose of getting two cows which he had purchased. The driver drove the truck to the barn by the way of the driveway, 6 feet in width. It was dark and the headlights were turned on. The driver testified he was driving about 7 miles per hour. He had been going to the premises to purchase cattle for approximately 15 years and knew of the presence of a dog on the farm. He testified he did not know the whereabouts of the dog. The driver did not see nor hear the dog and did not know such an accident had happened. The dog's body lay in the driveway and was found about a half hour after the truck driver had left. There was a judgment for the owner of the dog. The court said that it was fairly inferable from the evidence that the truck had passed over the head of the dog, killing it. If the driver of the truck had exercised due care, he would have observed the dog in time to avoid the collision; the requisite degree of care was not used in the operation of the vehicle under the circumstances prevailing at the time.

A motorist's liability for negligence in cases of animals on the highway is to be tested by the application of the standard of due care. And in the case of a dog the application of the standard of due care must be tested by the extent the driver of a motor vehicle on the highway or road may safely or properly rely upon the intelligence and agility of a dog to avoid a collision in the light of common experience. The degree of care required of the driver of a vehicle must be determined from the circumstance of each particular case.

The following cases are some examples of negligent acts sufficient to hold a driver of a motor vehicle liable for injuring or killing a dog.

In *Griffin* vs. *Fancher*, 127 Conn. 686, the Supreme Court was faced with the question of whether the owner of a registered dog may maintain an action for damages against one unintentionally but negligently killing or injuring the animal. The driver, while operating his automobile at a reasonable speed on the right-hand side of the street, ran over and killed a dog standing on the shoulder of the road at the edge of the traveled portion. The driver did not see the dog and was unaware of its presence until

he felt a bump caused by the right wheel of his car passing over it. The dog was duly licensed and was worth
$100. The trial court found for the owner of the dog, hold-
ing that the driver of the car failed to maintain a proper
lookout and failed to observe the dog and that such negligence was the proximate cause of the death of the animal.
The Supreme Court said that:

> Our common law is constantly in process of gradual but
> steady evolution. Because of more enlightened modern
> conceptions of the nature of dogs as animals and their
> value and status as property, we now decide, consonant
> with the weight of modern authority, that by our com-
> mon law there is a right of action against one who negli-
> gently kills or injures them, at least if they are properly
> registered. . . . Dogs are valuable, are subject to taxa-
> tion, and stealing them is put on a par with the larceny
> of any other personal property; this substantial property
> right should be accorded the same protection as other
> species of property . . . it would seem strange that a
> driver negligent by injuring a dog worth $100.00 stand-
> ing on the shoulder of the road would not be subject
> to an action for damages, but would be if he ran into
> a wheelbarrow. The propensity of dogs to roam is of
> significance, but is only a circumstance to be considered
> in deciding the question whether the injuring person
> was negligent. . . . The trial court's conclusion that the
> plaintiff (owner of the dog) could recover damages,
> under the facts of this case, for negligent killing of his
> registered dog, is correct.

At common law dogs are property and recovery can be
had by the owner where he proves the dog was killed by
the negligence of a driver of an automobile. In the states
where the owner is required to register the dog, failure

to register may prevent recovery. The same general rule applies to licensing dogs. The more modern concept and the weight of authority holds that an owner of a dog, licensed or unlicensed, may maintain an action for damages against any person or corporation willfully or negligently killing or injuring an animal, since the unlicensed dog is not a trespasser upon the public highway.

Two New York decisions are cases in point. The owner of a five-month-old Fox Terrier brought the dog to the street. The dog ran and played with the children and while in the street close to the curb a taxi killed the pup. The character of the area and the street was such as to call for caution on the part of operators of automobiles. Judgment was rendered in favor of the owner of the dog and the court said: "To take a pup from the household to the highway is a legitimate errand. To release it of its leash or muzzle is not in itself negligence. The ordinances requiring these precautions manifestly were adopted to protect the public from attack by the dog, not to protect the dog from assault by the public, naturally one cannot exact or expect of a dumb animal that standard of prudence that marks the conduct of the average careful creature. Aside from the question of negligence and contributory negligence, there is presented the question of damages. A live dog is personal property. Its value is governed by the type and traits and pedigree of the dog. What one pays for property is of importance in appraising its value, though not necessarily controlling."

The second case in point, the owner's dog was negligently run over and killed by the driver of a car. The driver claimed that the dog was running at large without a tag, basing his defense upon the law that provided that no action shall be maintained to recover the possession or value of a dog, or damages for injury or destruction of a dog, not wearing a tag attached to a collar. The question arose as to whether this provision was intended to protect officers against suits for injury or destruction of a dog caused while in performance of their duties, or whether it intended to permit any private individual to kill or injure an untagged dog without being liable in damages. The Court held that the law does not apply to persons who negligently run over and kill an untagged dog and is not a defense to this action. The statute that untagged dogs were to be seized and held showed that it was not the intention of the lawmakers to permit them to be killed when caught at large by individuals other than peace officers.

In states where an unregistered female running at large was declared by statute to be a public and common nuisance, the courts have held that even if a dog was a public nuisance it did not give a person the right to kill the dog when the dog was not molesting or attacking the person. A valuable female bird dog, which was unregistered and running at large, was killed by the driver of an automobile. Evidence was introduced at the trial to show there was nothing to prevent the driver from operating his car so as to miss the bird dog. The driver claimed since the statute made all unregistered female dogs running at large a public nuisance he was not liable for damages and had a right to intentionally abate the nuisance. Judgment was rendered for $100 in favor of the owner of the dog. The Court said that even if the dog was a public nuisance the driver of the car had no right to kill the dog when it was not molesting him. A person may abate a public nuisance only when suffering injury peculiar to himself; otherwise it is the function of the state officers to abate a nuisance.

We may sum up by saying that a driver of an automobile is liable if he negligently or willfully injures or kills a dog; dogs are not trespassers while on the highways; in most states owners of dogs may recover if their dog is injured or killed by the negligent or willful act of a driver of an automobile, even if the owner fails to register, obtain a tag, or pay the taxes on his dog. There are still some states which require the owner to comply with the statutes pertaining to licenses, registering and taxing of dogs before recovery is permitted. All dog owners, to be safe, should comply with all local statutory requirements; then should their dog be injured or killed by a negligent or willful driver, they can maintain an action for damages.

Willful Injuring and Killing of Dogs

To justify the intentional injury or killing of a dog it must be done in the protection of life, limb or property. In *Kolinski v. Klein*, 100 Conn. 127 (1923), Klein admitted he killed the Kolinski dog when it was about 25 feet from the Klein property, barking at him. Klein shot through the wire fence, killing the dog. It was clear that the killing was neither in the protection of life, limb or property. The Court found for the owner of the dog and held that Klein willfully and without justification killed the Kolinski dog.

In *Lowell v. Cathright*, 97 Ind. 313, the defendant contended that the owner of the dog could not recover because the dog at the time the defendant killed it was not wearing a metallic tag as required by statute and that

he had a right to kill it. The Court found that the dog
was unlawfully killed and that the law giving officers the
right to kill an untagged dog did not give other persons
the right. The defendant was not an officer; therefore, he
was liable if he killed a dog that was not running at large.

In Maryland the Court held that a landowner does not
have the right to kill trespassing dogs merely because they
are on his land.

Some states provide that it shall be lawful for any person to kill any dog for which a license is required, when
such dog is not wearing a collar with a license tag attached; others provide that police officers may kill any
dog found without a license tag.

Liability of Kennel Clubs and Superintendents

Kennel Clubs and superintendents promoting and sponsoring dog shows owe a duty to use reasonable care to
keep the premises safe for the public and the exhibitors.
The law uses the term of "foreseeability," which means
that if a reasonable, prudent member of a club or a superintendent could foresee the probability of a person being
injured by some act or omission, then the club or superintendent owes a duty to prevent the possibility of such
injury. For example, if the club or superintendent knew
of a vicious dog running loose at the show and failed to
catch the dog and confine it to prevent it from biting some
person attending the show, the club and the superintendent would be negligent, for the reason that the probable
consequences of permitting a vicious dog to run loose
would be that some person might be injured. If the club
or superintendent did not know that the dog was vicious,
then there would be no liability for failure to act. Through-

out, the courts hold that kennel clubs and superintendents must use reasonable and prudent care to protect the public.

A case in point is *Spalaine v. Eastern Dog Club*, 28 N.E.2d 450, (1950). Plaintiff entered a dog in the show and had paid the entry fee; one morning he brought his dog back to the show after having taken him home for the night. The dogs on exhibition were placed upon rows of benches or stalls with an aisle six feet wide between them. The plaintiff, on the morning in question, walked down the aisle with his dog, holding him by a chain or leash, toward the bench or stall allotted to this dog, and saw one O'Conner standing in the aisle talking with Lyons. O'Conner was showing dogs at the show. One of O'Conner's dogs bit the plaintiff. O'Conner jerked his dog loose and the dog grabbed the plaintiff's dog by the nose.

At the time the plaintiff was bitten, there were no attendants around and the superintendent was absent.

Club rules stated that all "dogs must be supplied with suitable collars and chains."

Court held:

Clearly it could have been found that the plaintiff was a business visitor of the defendant, The Eastern Dog Club, to whom that defendant owed the duty to use reasonable care to keep the premises reasonably safe for the plaintiff's use. Reasonable care to keep the premises reasonably safe for the plaintiff from harm from the dogs on exhibition was within the scope of that duty. There was, however, no breach of that duty on the part of the defendant that constituted negligence unless the plaintiff's injury was, in its general nature, the probable consequence of some act or omission for which the defendant was responsible.

There was no evidence, nor is there any contention, that

the plaintiff's injury was the consequence of any affirmative act of the defendant. The plaintiff's case against this defendant rests solely on the omission of the defendant to take reasonable precaution to guard against such an injury and the finding was not warranted that there was any such omission.

The presence of dogs on the premises was an essential feature of the show and it could not have been found that it was unreasonable to permit dogs to be taken through the aisles.

There was no evidence that before the occurrence in question the O'Conner dog had any dangerous propensities which were known or should have been known to the defendant or any other person.

Common law is that if such animal is rightfully in the place where the mischief is done, unless it appears that the animal is vicious and that this fact is known to the owner or keeper, there is no liability.

In the case of *Cruickshank v. Brockton*, Agr. Soc. 260 Mass. 283, the Court allowed a spectator to recover damages for injuries sustained when a dog bit her. The spectator had purchased a ticket of admission and entered the fairgrounds where dogs were exhibited. While viewing the dogs, in the space reserved for spectators, she was bitten by one of the dogs on exhibition, which, at the time of the injury, was held by its owner on a chain. The dog sprang from the bench and bit the spectator on the lip. The Court said that as an invitee, she could assume that the premises, aside from obvious dangers, were reasonably safe for the purposes for which they were arranged and adapted for the entertainment. Whether the dog was properly guarded and due precautions were taken by those operating the fair to protect spectators from being molested were questions for the jury. The evidence disclosed that the chain holding the dog was five feet long—long enough to permit the dog to reach spectators standing in the space reserved for them. Based on this evidence, the jury could find that such injury might reasonably have been anticipated.

The law imposes a duty upon an owner, club or superintendent to exercise reasonable care—or the care of an ordinary prudent person—to prevent dogs from inflicting any injury which may reasonably be anticipated, in view of all the circumstances.

Those who operate and sponsor dog shows are not insurers of the safety of the patrons, and it is their duty to render the place in which they hold shows reasonably safe to all persons lawfully in attendance, and they are liable for injuries to invitees sustained by reason of failure to do so. It is an active duty to guard against all risks which may reasonably be anticipated.

Legal Obligation of a Handler and Owner of Boarding Kennels: General.

Since dogs are personal property and a delivery of the dog is involved in both the handler and boarding kennel arrangements, the law of bailment generally applies. Bailment is defined as a delivery of personal property to another for certain purposes agreed upon by the parties, upon the understanding the property will be redelivered to the owner after the purposes have been fulfilled. For example, the owner of a dog delivers his animal to the handler for the purpose of training and showing the dog, or to a boarding kennel for the purpose of boarding the dog. In order to constitute a bailment, there must be a transfer of possession of the animal, the title to remain in the owner, with the understanding that the animal will be returned as agreed upon. There is also a term used in dealing with cattle, horses, sheep and the like when the owner desires to deliver the animals to another for pasturing and feeding. The law of "agistment" also applies in the broad general terms. But due to the many peculiar problems involving the boarding kennels, careful consideration must be given to principles of law applying to agistments.

The owner of the personal property is called the "bailor." One who receives the property for a specific purpose is called the "bailee." To understand the Court's decisions, one must keep in mind that the owner of the dog would therefore be the "bailor." The handler or the owner of the boarding kennel would be the "bailee."

In general the bailee for hire must exercise ordinary care for the protection of the property in his custody; that is, such care as prudent men would ordinarily use toward their own property under similar circumstances. Whether he used ordinary care under all the circumstances of the case is a question for a jury. A bailee is bound to exercise ordinary diligence for the safety of the animals entrusted to his care. The bailee is not liable as an insurer in the absence of a special agreement. He is bound to exercise ordinary diligence in keeping, feeding, sheltering and otherwise caring for the animals entrusted to him. He is not liable for injury or loss occurring without his fault.

Liability for Acts of Dog Kept by Handler or Boarding Kennel

Generally speaking, a person who keeps a dog for another, such as in boarding kennels and handlers, is not liable for damages in instances where injuries are inflicted by a dog he does not own. However, there is an exception to the general rule. The Supreme Court of California stated the exception. "A keeper is not an insurer of the good behavior of a dog, but must have scienter or knowledge of vicious propensities of the animal before liability for injuries inflicted by such animal shall attach to him." In this case the Court rules on the "Dog Bite Statute" by holding that a statute imposing liability on the owner of a dog without regard to knowledge of his vicious nature does not apply to one merely harboring or keeping a dog not owned by him; and in order to render him liable, previous knowledge of the dog's vicious nature must appear.

So where a statute makes only the owner liable, the general law of bailment applies. In those states having Dog Bite Statutes, it is important to determine if liability is limited only to the owner or to the keeper as well.

However, in those states where the "Dog Bite Statute" makes the owner or the keeper liable for damages caused by a dog in his care, the handler and boarding kennel owner cannot rely on the law of bailment. The handler and boarding kennel owner would be bound by the same rules of law as set forth under "Statutory Liability."

5

The Veterinarian

Malpractice.

A veterinarian does not, in the absence of a special contract to do so, undertake to perform a cure of dogs he treats. He only agrees to use such reasonable skill, diligence and attention as may be expected of the careful, skillful, ordinary attention possessed by a veterinarian in the community where he practices. In other words, a veterinarian does not undertake the treatment of a dog at the hazard of an action for damages if he fails to effect a cure or produce a perfect result. He is not an insurer of favorable consequences as the result of a particular treatment or operation which he has recommended or performed. The same rule that applies to medical doctors applies to veterinarians. *Rasmussen v. Shickle*, 41 Pac. (2) 184 contains the general rule:

"The law does not require that the advice, instructions and treatment given by a physician to a patient shall be at all events proper, or that his treatment should be such as to attain an approximate perfect result. It requires only, first, that he shall have the degree of learning and skill ordinarily possessed by physicians of good standing practicing in that locality; and, second, that he shall exercise reasonable and ordinary care and diligence in treating the patient and in applying such learning and skill to the case."

It will be noted that the above quotation requires a veterinarian to use reasonable and ordinary care, the same as a physician or surgeon. The same general legal principles apply to both the medical doctor and the veterinarian.

In the case of *Kerbow v. Bell*, 259 P. 317 (Okl.), damages were sought by the owner of a dog for the loss of his pet, which died soon after being dipped by the defendant (veterinarian) in a lye solution as a cure for mange. In the trial another veterinarian testified the solution used was too strong and death could have resulted therefrom. The Court held a person professing and undertaking to treat animals is bound to use, in performing the duties of his employment, such reasonable skill, diligence and attention as may ordinarily be expected of careful, skillful and trustworthy persons in his profession, and if he does not possess and exercise these qualities, he is answerable for the result of his want of skill and care.

In *Carson v. City of Beloit*, 145 N.W.2d 112 (Wis., Oct. 7, 1966) the Court held a veterinarian not liable for death of puppies. "Damages could not be recovered in a suit against a veterinarian for the death of five pedigreed puppies, where the evidence failed to show that the veterinarian was negligent in his treatment of them," a Louisiana intermediate appellate court ruled.

One of the puppies was admitted to the veterinarian's clinic because of labored breathing, abdominal pains, and other symptoms. After various tests and examinations, he diagnosed the condition as tapeworms and coccidia. For the next two weeks, the puppy was alternately given supportive treatment and, when its physical condition warranted, sulfa-quanadine, the proper treatment for coccidia. The puppy died at the end of this period, and the postmortem showed signs of coccidia. A veterinarian who testified for the owner stated that he could not say that the puppy's death would not have occurred if a different treatment had been given. Thus, there was no basis for holding the veterinarian liable for the death of this puppy.

About two months after the puppy died, the mother was brought to the veterinarian's clinic because she had a fever and her appetite was poor. Examinations and tests disclosed that she had abscessed anal glands, pharyngitis, otitis, conjunctivitis, and metritis. She was discharged after 10 days of treatment. The next day, another veterinarian examined the mother and diagnosed her condition as distemper. He made the same diagnosis as to the four remaining puppies. The puppies subsequently died. The owner contended that the veterinarian against whom this suit was brought was liable for the puppies' death, because he had negligently failed to diagnose the mother's distemper, she had transmitted the disease to them, and it had caused their death.

Expert witnesses for the owner stated that the veterinarian had used the degree of skill ordinarily used by members of the profession in good standing in the community. The doctrine of *res ipsa loquitur* was not applicable. The doctrine did not apply because a question of diagnosis and treatment requiring professional judgment was involved, the court said. Further, nothing unusual occurred during the veterinarian's treatment of the mother from which a presumption of negligence could arise, and he did not treat the four puppies.

Incorrect Diagnosis and Treatment

In making examinations to diagnose the ailment of an animal the question for the Court to determine is whether the veterinarian did the things necessary to conform to the standards of his profession in his community.

A veterinarian, once he has undertaken to examine a dog who is apparently sick, is under duty to exercise the ordinary care as established by the standards of veterinary medicine in his community. The gist of such action is the failure to properly diagnose the sickness. Often the question may be one of judgment, and liability should not follow a mistake of judgment. If two or more veterinarians have different opinions as to the ailment, it is a matter of judgment; there can be no negligence. A veterinarian will be liable for gross ignorance and want of skill. He does not contract to use the highest degree of skill nor an extraordinary amount of diligence.

A veterinarian who undertakes to render professional services must meet these requirements: (1) He must possess the degree of professional learning, skill and ability which others similarly situated ordinarily possess; (2) he must exercise reasonable care and diligence in the application of his knowledge and skill to the patient's case; and (3) he must use his best judgment in the treatment and care of his patient. If the veterinarian lives up to the foregoing requirements he is not civilly liable for the consequences. If he fails in any one particular, and such failure is the proximate cause of injury and damage, he is liable.

Action will lie against a veterinary surgeon for gross ignorance and want of skill as well as for negligence.

A veterinarian who undertakes to treat an animal may be liable for negligence in treatment notwithstanding the fact that such undertaking was gratuitous. He does not relieve himself merely by not charging for his services.

Liable for Acts of Agent or Employees

A veterinarian may be liable for the negligent acts of his agent or employees. In the case of *Acherman v. Robertson*, 3 N.W.(2) 723 (Wis.), the owner of 89 hogs brought suit for damages after his hogs died due to the spraying of the hogs with lysol, under the belief that the product was mange oil. The owner alleged that the lysol was negligently delivered to him by the veterinarian's son in place of the mange oil he had ordered. The veterinarian's son, who had two years of training in veterinary practice, helped his father in and about the office. The veterinarian had told the owner about the mange oil and that they could get some any time at his office. The owner called while the veterinarian was away, and the son got a can labeled "Liquor Cresolis Sapanetus." The son thought the Liquor Cresolis Sapanetus was the Latin term for "mange oil." The son delivered the can to the owner. The owner sprayed his hogs without reading the label. Soon the hogs were dead.

The Court held that the son was the agent of his father. The son was negligent in delivering the can of lysol instead of the mange oil. The veterinarian therefore was liable for the act of his agent.

It is a fundamental rule of agency law that the principal is bound by, and liable for, those acts which his agent does within the actual or apparent authority of the principal, and those acts which the agent does within the scope of his employment. When a veterinarian permits another to act for him and a third party justifiably relies upon the care and skill of such agent or employee and the third person is harmed by the lack of care or skill of the servant, agent or employee, the veterinarian is liable.

Employment Contract Between Veterinarians

Professional people such as veterinarians often enter into partnership agreements and employment contracts which provide that in the event of the termination of the contract, one of the parties agrees not to engage in the practice of their profession for a certain period of time and not to practice within certain areas. The provisions of the agreement are known as restrictive covenants. The courts have held that public policy favors enforcement of contracts intended to protect legitimate interests and frowns upon unreasonable restrictions. The following two cases will help to illustrate these two views.

The case of *Brecher v. Brown*, 17 N.W. (2) 377, involved a suit for injunction to restrain the defendant from the practice of veterinary medicine and surgery and the operation of a veterinary hospital in violation of the terms of a contract of employment.

On March 25, 1943, the parties executed a written agreement by which the plaintiff employed the defendant as a veterinary assistant in Storm Lake, Iowa, for an indefinite period of time at a salary of $200 per month until changed by further agreement. Defendant agreed not to engage in any other type of work and to devote all his working hours to plaintiff's service. The controversy involved the following paragraph of the contract:

"It is further stipulated and agreed that upon the termination of the second party's employment by the first party that the second party will not engage in the practice of veterinary medicine or surgery, or any competing business of that of first party, in Storm Lake, Iowa, or a territory within a radius of twenty-five miles of Storm Lake, Iowa, without the expressed written consent of first party." Both parties were licensed veterinarians. Plaintiff operated a veterinary hospital in connection with his practice.

They operated under the agreement until December 27, 1943, when defendant quit and soon thereafter opened a veterinary office and hospital about 100 feet from plaintiff's office and hospital.

The Court held:

Under earlier decisions, the Courts held that restrictions unlimited as to both time and space were invalid; those limited as to time but unlimited as to space were also held invalid; while those limited as to space but unlimited as to time and those limited as to both time and space were ordinarily upheld.

It has been held that restrictive stipulations in agreements between employer and employee are not viewed with the same indulgence as such stipulations between a vendor and vendee of a business and its good will.

We are constrained to agree with the trial court that the area attempted to be reserved by the appellant (plaintiff) is much greater than reasonably necessary to his protection. The fact he has a patron twenty-six miles away and others somewhat less remote does not fix the area of his practice as a circle with a twenty-five mile radius.

The restriction is entirely unlimited as to time and has

no relationship to duration of the employment which the contract expressly made indefinite.

The indefiniteness in the time and employment does not render the contractual restriction without consideration, but it is to be taken into account in appraising the reasonableness of the restriction which was entirely unlimited in duration.

In the case of *Beam v. Rutledge*, 9 S.E. (2) 476, Beam, in a civil action against Rutledge to enjoin him from practice of medicine in violation of an agreement entered into by the parties in which the following clause was in the partnership agreement, is the one causing the controversy:

In the event of a dissolution of the co-partnership herein created, it is agreed by Dr. H. M. Rutledge, one of the parties, that he will not engage in the practice of the profession of medicine in the Town of Lumberton, Robeson County, North Carolina, or within 100 miles of said Town of Lumberton, Robeson County, North Carolina, for a period of five years from the date of said dissolution.

Partnership was dissolved and Rutledge opened an office in the Town of Lumberton. There was but a single question for the Court to decide. Whether the restrictive covenant in the partnership agreement was valid and enforceable.

The application of two principles were involved here: freedom to contract and public policy. The plaintiff invoked the one, the defendant the other.

Speaking of public policy, the Court said that this contract is not forbidden by any principle of policy or law. A doctor can be useful to the public at any other town as in the town where he is now presently practicing, and the lives and health of persons in other villages are as important as they are here. Communities are, therefore, not injured by any stipulation of this kind between two practicing and eminent physicians.

The Court discussed freedom of contract by saying the right of the parties to decide upon what terms and conditions they are willing to form a partnership, or to enter into a contract of the character here disclosed, is not to be lightly abridged. Indeed, it is no small part of the liberty of citizens. The parties themselves, when the contract was made, regarded the restriction as reasonable. They were dealing with a situation of which both were familiar. The defendant insisted on having the contract signed and did not object to the restrictive covenant. It was limited both as to time and place.

The important thing to remember is that the restrictive covenant must be limited in time and place. If the contract is unlimited as to years, the Court will hold it void and of no effect. The same thing is true if there is no limit as to the territory the party is restricted to in the practice of his profession.

Even though the contract is limited as to time and place, it can be void because of unreasonableness as to time and place. The Court held in the above case that five years was not unreasonable, nor the restriction of 100 miles. Reasonableness of these two important principles depend upon the facts of each case. If a physician's patients were limited to 100 mile radius, it would be unreasonable for the agreement to provide a restrictive covenant limiting the practice within 200 miles.

Action for Services Rendered

Whenever it becomes necessary for a veterinarian to bring action to collect his fee for services rendered, he must allege that he is a veterinarian and that he held himself out as such, also that he is a licensed veterinarian under the laws of the state where he is practicing, as one Court said: It requires education to be able to treat diseases of dumb animals, as well as diseases of man. There is no presumption of qualification. It is equally essential that he should establish it by proof. If he were simply a "quack" without education or experience, and were employed by the owner of the dog upon the representation that he was a qualified veterinarian, he could not recover. Proof that the services were reasonable and necessary to treat the dog is a necessary item of proof. A Court in New York said: "Doubtless the same rules are applicable to the case of a veterinary surgeon bringing an action to recover the value of his services, as have been applicable to other physicians and surgeons. He must possess and exercise a reasonable degree of learning and skill. He must use reasonable and ordinary care and diligence in the exercise of his skill and the application of his knowledge." Otherwise he could not recover.

6

The Carrier's Liability for Injury and Loss of Dogs

In general it is the duty of a common carrier, in the transporting of animals, to use that degree of care and prudence that an ordinary person would use under the same or similar circumstances to transport them to their destination; the carrier is liable for the failure to use such care to protect the animals from any form of violence or improper handling which would tend to injure them, but it is not liable for any injuries resulting merely from the ordinary and proper operation of the train, truck or transportation vehicle. By permitting animals to be exposed to excessive heat or cold for long periods of time, with the result that the animals suffer death or injury, the carrier would be liable.

If any animal injures itself without fault on the part of the carrier and the carrier fails to exercise the reasonable care necessary to prevent its subsequent death, the carrier is liable. The owner of an animal must prove that the carrier's negligent acts were the proximate result of the injury or death of the animal. When animals are shown to have been delivered to the carrier in good condition, and to have been injured on the way, the burden then

111

rests on the carrier to show that death or injury was not caused by the carrier's own negligence.

In the case of *Southern Express Company v. McClellan*, 66 Colo. 591, 185 Pac. 347 (1919), there was an action to recover for the loss of a dog shipped in a crate from South Carolina to Colorado. The crate contained directions to the express company's (the carrier's) messengers to exercise the dog at least once a day. This was not done and the dog was removed from the crate at no time. On the fourth day, the dog died. He died from peritonitis from a ruptured bladder, which the dog, being housebroken, had declined to empty while in the crate. In affirming the judgment for the owner of the dog, the Court said:

> The express company contends that the shipper's directions called by the rules of the Interstate Commerce Commission, and that therefore, the defendant could not, and was not required to comply with such directions. In our opinion, the instructions in question did not demand a special service. It called for nothing more than certain care of an animal while in transit, and no unreasonable degree of attention or service was necessary in order to obey the instructions. No statute nor regulation has been pointed out which relieves the carrier, as a common carrier, of the unusual responsibility of care for animals, delivered to it for transportation, while the same are in transit. The fact that the carrier could not make a charge for service, unless such charge is provided for in the published tariffs and classifications, does not affect the existence of the duty to render such service as is necessary to the proper care of livestock in transit. We find nothing in the record to take the care out of the rule which makes it the duty of the carrier to follow shipping directions.

When a carrier deviates from the stipulated route, he becomes an insurer, and responsible for all loss and damages to the goods, even unavoidable casualty.

In *Ely v. Barrett*, 181 App. Div. 176, 168 NYS 419, the owner of a dog brought action to recover for the death of a dog shipped by express from New York to California. The shipper instructed defendant (railroad) what lines to send it over, but the railroad disregarded these instructions and sent the dog over its own lines to a place in Ohio, where it was found dead. Owner had verdict and judgment.

In the written decision the Court said:

The plaintiff's contention is that by reason of the deviation from the stipulated route the defendant is liable for the loss as insurer; while the defendant's theory is that the carrier at common law does not insure against the consequences of the vitality of live freight, but is liable only for the results of its own negligence, that the parties have so stipulated in the form filed with the Interstate Commerce Commission, and that to allow a departure from such agreement would be a discrimination condemned by the Interstate Commerce Act . . . .

In the contract the shipper releases the carrier—"from all liability for delay, injuries to or loss of said animals, . . . from any cause whatever, unless such delay, injury, or loss shall be caused by the express company or by the negligence of its agent and employees . . . ."

The stipulation means that in the course of the specific service undertaken the carrier shall be liable for the loss caused by its negligence proven by the shipper. That put the burden of proof upon the shipper. But the carrier in fact departed materially from the agreement, and assumed to carry the dog by another route, for an increased distance under its immediate care and control, in a different territory, per chance under different climatic conditions, for delivery to a different connecting carrier, and in the course of such carriage the animal died. Do such facts relieve the shipper from further evidence that the death was caused by some act of defendant done or omitted, and imposed upon the carrier the burden of showing, not only due care, but also that the changed route did not enhance the risk of loss? I am at the moment dealing merely with the effect of the deviation on the burden of proof of negligence. It was something more than negligence to divert the carriage from the Wells Fargo Express at New York. . . .

The stipulated facts show the following report by the express messenger: "This dog was lying down in crate when received at Pittsburgh. Would not get up when loaded in the car, and appeared to be sick. I placed her near the door to get air, and gave her feed and water; but she would neither eat nor drink, and would not get up when I spoke to her. As she did not appear to be suffering, I thought she was all right. I looked in crate again after leaving Pittsburgh. She was still lying down. After leaving Wooster, Ohio, I examined her again and found she was dead."

What delay or exposure attended the diversion, where or under what conditions the sickness appeared, what was overlooked, if not beyond plaintiff's ascertainment, although presumptively within the knowledge of the erring carrier, were at least things that the shipper did not agree to prove. Moreover, when the dog was "loaded in the car" at Pittsburgh she was sick, and yet without rest she was sent forward. I think that the court was quite justified in finding that the defendant was negligent.

But the usual rule is that, when a carrier deviates from the stipulated route, he becomes an insurer, and responsible for all loss and damage to the goods, even unavoidable casualty. . . .

7

Dogs and Income Taxes

In determining whether the training, showing and breeding of dogs will be considered a business or a hobby in the eyes of the Internal Revenue will depend upon several factors. If it is considered a business, expenses are deductible as in any other business. If it is a hobby, expenses are not deductible. Yet, profits are taxable. Therefore, it is most important to be able to prove you intend to produce a profit and that such enterprise should be considered a trade or business. There can be a very thin line separating a hobby from a business. Some hobbies become profitable. They become a business. There are certain guidelines to distinguish those qualifying for expense and loss deductions. The courts have held that raising and breeding animals may well be an enterprise entered into as a business for profit. The burden is on the taxpayer to prove it is a trade or business and not a hobby.

Documention of all your records is most important, for evidence that the taxpayer entered the breeding, showing or training of dogs with a sincere effort to make a profit. Here the intent of the taxpayer is of paramount importance. Some of the factors in determining if the breeding, showing or training of dogs is a business rather than a hobby are as follows: (1) Taxpayers' personal attention to phases of the operation and a practical and common sense managing such as would be expected in any other business enterprise. (2) Serious study and acquired knowledge going into the operation. Functional kennel design with no attempt to make it a show place. (3) Advertisement and promotion of stud dogs and marketing dogs in dog magazines. (4) A kennel enterprise of such size that there is a reasonable opportunity to gain a profit. (5) A well-planned program of breeding and marketing that will show a profit in four or five years. (6) The operation of the kennel and showing and the breeding of dogs is the only occupation. (7) The keeping of complete records of all transactions. (8) After a reasonable time there must be a profit.

It requires time to build up any kind of business. The dog business is not unlike the beginning orchardist who plants trees and waits several years for even the first crop to be harvested.

A federal court set forth several points in determining if the enterprise is a hobby or a business: (1) The taxpayer's intention is the determining factor as to whether the enterprise's losses are deductible as a business entered into for profit. (2) Whether the dog business is a hobby or a business depends upon the circumstances of each case. The seven factors listed above are some of the circumstances which will help to prove the enterprise is business or trade. (3) If the taxpayer has independent income and the amount of money expended each year would put the average kennel owner or the average handler out of business, this fact tends to show a hobby. (4) Last, but the most important rule governing such cases, is the rule that the burden of proof that the taxpayer is carrying on a business enterprise for a profit is upon the taxpayer. This means that you must come forth with sufficient facts, records, and evidence to convince the court of your intent. Each case must be treated on its own merits, since no two cases are identical.

Section 61 of the United States Internal Revenue Code defines taxable income as gross income minus deductions and Section 162 provides for deductions of ordinary and necessary expenses of a trade or business. The question is how the courts define "business." The courts endeavor to find out from the evidence the taxpayer presents, if the enterprise is for a personal pleasure or an undertaking established for a profit.

In the event a taxpayer is questioned as to his deductions and losses in operating a dog business he should be prepared to show from his own testimony and from records that there is a reasonable expectation of making a profit. This requires tax planning from the beginning of the business. There is no substitute for well-documented records. Professional handlers will have very little difficulty in showing they are in the business of handling and showing dogs for a profit. The difficulty arises most often when a businessman operates a kennel as a sideline while spending full time in his business or profession.

Appendix:
Forms You Will Encounter as a Dog Owner

Agreement to Handle and Show Dogs

THIS AGREEMENT, Made and entered into this _____ day of _____, 19__, by and between _____, of _____, hereinafter called the "Handler" and _____, of _____, hereinafter called the "Owner".

WITNESSETH:

WHEREAS, the owner owns a certain _____(sex), _____(breed) dog, named _____, A. K. C. Registration Number _____, age _____ years and is desirous of having the said dog trained and shown, and

WHEREAS, the Handler is licensed by the A.K.C. as a dog handler experienced in training and showing pure-bred dogs and is desirous of showing said dog,

NOW, THEREFORE, in consideration of the mutual covenants and agreements herein contained the parties agree as follows:

1. The owner agrees to deliver one registered _____(sex), _____(breed) dog named _____, A. K. C. Registration Number _____ to the Handler at _____(address) to be trained and shown.

2. The Handler shall have the right to select dog shows where the said dog is to be shown. The Handler shall

notify the owner when the dog is entered in a show either by mail, wire or telephone and shall notify the owner the results of same by the same method.

3. The owner shall, during the term of this agreement, pay the Handler as follows:

(a) $_____ each show.

(b) $_____ for each first place group win.

(c) $_____ for each best in show.

(d) $_____ a day board.

In addition the owner shall pay for all long distance telephone calls, wires, entry fees and all medical bills. Payment shall be made within ten (10) days after billing (or on the _____ day of each month beginning on the _____ day of _____, 19____.)

4. The Handler agrees to train and show the above described dog and to feed and care for it in a good and proper manner as is necessary in preparing and maintaining the said dog in show shape.

5. Transportation of the dog to and from dog shows shall be provided by the Handler.

6. It is agreed that the dog shall be listed in the name of the owner and handled in the name of the Handler.

7. In the event the dog becomes ill or in need of major medical attention or hospital attention, the Handler shall notify the Owner by telephone or wire for instructions.

8. Either party may terminate this agreement by notifying the other in writing or by wire as first above written. The Handler shall return the dog to the Owner or his agent and in accordance with instructions of the Owner. They shall pay to the Handler the amount due at time of redelivery of the dog to the Owner or his agent.

9. All prize money shall belong to (Handler) (Owner) and the ribbons and trophies shall belong to the Owner.

10. The Handler shall use his best efforts in training and showing said dog.

This Agreement is signed and executed on this the
_____ day of _____, 19____, in duplicate.

(Handler)_____

(Owner)_____

Agreement to Handle and Show a Dog at Specific Show

THIS AGREEMENT, Made and entered into this _____ day
of _____, 19____, by and between _____, of _____,
hereinafter called the "Handler" and _____, of _____,
hereinafter called the "Owner",

WITNESSETH:

WHEREAS, the owner owns a certain _____(sex),
_____(breed), dog named _____, A.K.C. Registration
Number _____, age _____ years and is desirous of
having the said dog trained and shown, and

WHEREAS, the Handler is licensed by the A.K.C. as a
dog handler experienced in training and showing pure
bred dogs and is desirous of showing said dog,

NOW, THEREAFTER, in consideration of the mutual covenants and agreements herein contained, the parties agree
as follows:

1. The Owner agrees to deliver one registered
_____(sex), _____(breed) dog named _____, A.K.C.
Registration Number _____ to the Handler at
_____(address) to be trained and shown.

2. The Handler shall show the said dog at the following shows:

1.

2.

3.

4.

and such other shows as the Owner shall select in writing
to the Handler.

3. The owner shall, during the term of this agreement, pay the Handler as follows:

(a) $____ each show.

(b) $____ for each first place group win.

(c) $____ for each best in show.

(d) $____ a day board.

In addition the owner shall pay for all long distance telephone calls, wires, entry fees and all medical bills. Payment shall be made within ten (10) days after billing (or on the ____ day of each month beginning on the ____ day of _____, 19____).

4. The Handler agrees to train and show the above described dog and to feed and care for it in a good and proper manner as is necessary in preparing and maintain the said dog in show shape.

5. Transportation of the dog to and from dog shows shall be provided by the Handler.

6. It is agreed that the dog shall be listed in the name of the owner and handled in the name of the Handler.

7. In the event the dog becomes ill or in need of major medical attention or hospital attention, the Handler shall notify the Owner by telephone or wire for instructions.

8. Either party may terminate this agreement by notifying the other in writing or by wire as first above written. The Handler shall return the dog to the Owner or his agent and in accordance with instructions of the Owner. They shall pay to the Handler the amount due at time of re-delivery of the dog to the Owner or his agent.

9. All prize money shall belong to (Handler) (Owner) and the ribbons and trophies shall belong to the Owner.

10. The andler shall use his best efforts in training and showing said dog.

This Agreement is signed and executed on this the ____ day of _____, 19____, in duplicate.

(Handler)_____

(Owner)_____

Boarding Kennel Agreement

DATE_____

NAME OF OWNER:_____

ADDRESS _____

HOME PHONE _____ BUSINESS PHONE _____

BREED OF DOG _____ AGE _____ SEX _____

APPROXIMATE WEIGHT _____LBS. SPECIAL MARKS OR

SCORES _____. OBVIOUS DEFECTS _____

_____

VET'S NAME _____

PHONE _____ SPECIAL SERVICE ORDERS _____

_____

DISPOSITION OF DOG _____

The owner agrees to:

1. Pay in advance $____ per (day)(week)(month) as board.

2. Pay all medical, hospital and veterinarian expenses.

3. If the animal becomes ill or is injured, the owner shall be notified at once at owner's expense for instructions, and if owner cannot be informed or does not answer the notice or the dog's health requires immediate action, the kennel owner shall have the right to use his best judgment in regarding measures to be taken for the welfare and health of the dog.

4. The kennel shall not be liable for any damage which may accrue from any cause growing out of or as a result of the boarding of the said dog including but not limited to loss by fire, theft, running away, death, injury to person or dogs or property except gross negligence of the kennel, its agents, servants, and employees and then the liability of the kennel shall not exceed the sum of $____.

5. The kennel shall have and is hereby granted a lien on the aforesaid amount for any and all unpaid boarding and other charges resulting from boarding of said dog.

The owner shall pay for the boarding charges within _____ days after they become due and payable.

6. Kennel may exercise its lien rights and _____ days after written notice to the owner at the address above set out may dispose of said dog for the unpaid charges at private or public sale and the owner waives all other legal notice. In the event sale does not secure a price sufficient to pay costs and charges, the owner shall be liable for the difference. Any sum realized over and above costs and charges shall belong to the owner.

7. Owner agrees to abide by all the rules and regulations of the kennel in regard to visiting hours and check out time.

8. In the event some one other than the owner calls for the dog, such person shall have written authority signed by the owner to obtain the dog.

9. It is understood that the word "owner" means the owner of the dog and the word "kennel" means the owner and operator of the Boarding Kennel. No person is authorized to change or alter the terms of this agreement signed in duplicate.

_____(Owner or authorized agent)

Boarding Kennel

By _____

Bill of Sale Without Warranty

TO WHOM IT MAY CONCERN:

Know all men by these presents, that I, _____ of _____(address), have this day sold to _____(name), _____(address) a _____(sex) _____(breed) dog whelped on the _____(date), A.K.C. Registration Number _____ for the sum of _____($___) Dollars, the receipt whereof is hereby acknowledged.

IN WITNESS WHEREOF, I have hereunto set my hand and

seal this _____ day of _____, 19____, at _____(city),
_____(state).

_____(Seller) (SEAL)

Bill of Sale Stud Dog With Warranty

KNOW ALL MEN BY THESE PRESENTS:

That I, _____, of _____, have this day sold to
_____, of _____, a _____(sex), _____(breed) dog,
whelped on the _____(date whelped), A.K.C. Registration Number _____, for the sum of _____($____)
Dollars, the receipt whereof is hereby acknowledged.

In the event that the above named stud dog is properly used, and with bitches in good health and condition, I warrant that he has breeding capacity; but it is expressly provided, as a condition of this warranty, the purchaser shall keep a list of all bitches bred with the date of such service, name of owner and name and A.K.C. Number of bitches for one year from date of purchases.

In the event that the above conditions are not performed or should the above named dog hereafter become injured or disabled through accident or disease, this warranty shall be null and void and of no effect, and all obligations incurred by me herein shall be considered fulfilled and ended.

This bill of sale contains all the agreements of warranty or guaranty made by me in this sale.

IN WITNESS WHEREOF, I have hereunto set my hand and seal this the _____ day of _____, 19____.

_____(Seller) (SEAL)

Kennel Manager Contract

THIS AGREEMENT, Made this _____ day of _____, 19____,
by and between _____, hereinafter called the Owner,
and _____, hereinafter called the Manager,

WITNESSETH: _____ owns and operates a Kennel known as _____, and located at _____, and is desirous of employment of a full time Manager and _____ is experienced in the management of Kennels and the care of dogs.

Therefore, for and in consideration of the mutual covenants herein contained, the parties agree as follows:

1. The Manager, after inspecting the _____ Kennel and understanding the work involved, agrees to manage the Kennel for a period of ____ years, beginning on the ____day of _____, 19____, and terminating on the ____ day of _____, 19____.

2. The Manager shall devote his full time and best efforts in managing the said Kennel.

3. Manager shall contract no debts on account of the owner without first obtaining the sanction of the Owner.

4. All sums received from services performed by the Manager and employees shall belong to the Owner and adequate records shall be kept at all times.

5. Manager shall comply with all rules and regulations set forth in writing by the Owner for the operation of the Kennel.

6. In the event the Manager is required to travel on behalf of the Kennel, he shall be reimbursed for his actual expenses.

7. All records shall be open and available for examination at any time by the Owner.

8. The Owner shall furnish the Manager the following: (Here set forth living quarters, cars, etc., to be furnished to the Manager by the Owner.)

9. The Owner shall pay the Manager the sum of $____ per (week) (month), payable on:

(a) ____ day of each week.

(b) First and Fifteenth of each month.

(c) First of each month.

(d) or any other time as agreed upon between the parties.

10. Manager shall be entitled to ____ weeks vacation with pay each year, beginning after one year's employment.

Lease Agreement With Option to Buy

THIS LEASE executed this ____ day of _____, 19____, by and between _____, hereinafter referred to as "Owner," and _____, hereinafter referred to as "Lessee";

WITNESSETH: Owner does hereby lease to Lessee and Lessee does hereby lease from Owner for a period of ____ Months, approximately, beginning the ____ day of _____, 19____ and ending the ____ day of _____, 19____, the following animal:

RENTAL: The Lessee agrees to pay Owner a total sum of $____ for the use of the above dog for the lease period to be paid, _____. In addition, the Lessee agrees to pay the Owner the sum of _____ on or before _____, 19____, which will be refunded to the Lessee when he returns the dog to the Owner at his _____at the termination of this lease period providing the dog is in good condition (approximately the same condition as when accepted by the Lessee at the beginning of the lease period). Owner also hereby grants the Lessee the option to lease the dog for a second lease period to commence the day following the expiration date of this lease and the second lease period to end on or before the ____ day of _____, 19____, for a total sum of _____ to be paid, $____ the day second lease period starts (_____) and $____ on or before the ____ day of _____, 19____. Owner also grants Lessee option to purchase this dog for a total sum of $____ and if Lessee does purchase dog, the lease fee which has already been paid, (will) (will not) apply against the total of _____. To exercise either of these options, Lessee must notify Owner in writing to that effect on or before the ____ day of _____, 19____.

Lessee warrants that he(has) (has not) inspected said dog and agrees to accept this dog in his present condition. Lessee shall pay and provide for the transportation of the dog from Owner to the Lessee and for the return of said dog to Owner at _____ at the expiration of the Lease. Lessee shall not obligate owner for any expense of any kind whatsoever in connection with the leased dog unless authorized in writing by the Owner.

CARE OF DOG: The Lessee, at his expense, shall provide feed, service, equipment and other necessary services for the proper care, maintenance, handling and protection of the leased dog, also Veterinary services if needed, all according to the rules of good animal husbandry and reasonable standards and methods of the dog-breeding industry. Owner shall have the right at any time, in person or by authorized agent, to go upon the Lessee's premises to inspect the dog, and to determine if it has been properly cared for and in good health.

It is not necessary that Lessee provide death and injury insurance on the leased dog providing he provides good and reasonable care and precautions at all times to prevent injury or death of the dog, and providing if dog becomes sick or injured that Lessee immediately provides for proper veterinary care and attention at Lessee's expense. Owner will not hold Lessee liable for any serious injury or death of the dog while in custody of the Lessee.

The Lessee agrees to provide proper Veterinary care immediately at his expense, if the dog becomes sick or injured. The Lessee agrees to carry death and injury insurance on this dog in the amount of _____ with the loss payable to the Owner.

Owner will supply Lessee with such pedigree and registration information as may be needed for registration of future produce of this dog resulting from breeding him to bitches by the Lessee during this lease period. Lessee may stand at Stud the leased dog. Any stud fees collected by the Lessee during the lease period will be the property of _____.

Lessee shall hold Owner harmless for any injury to persons or damages to any property caused by this leased dog. Lessee shall not permit the leased dog to be seized or impounded by anyone because of damages to property of others. Lessee shall pay when due any taxes which may be levied by any city, township, county, state or other taxing body wherein said leased dog may be located during the term of said lease. Lessee shall not assign this lease nor sublease this dog covered hereby.

The title and ownership of the leased dog shall be and remain in the name of Owner. Lessee shall not sell, mortgage or encumber in any manner whatsoever this leased dog.

If the leased dog should at anytime become missing, lost, estrayed, seriously injured, sick, or dead, the Lessee shall immediately notify Owner by telephone and subsequently by mail. There shall be no abatement of rental paid due to death of leased dog if the dog dies during the period for which the rental has already been paid.

MODIFICATION OF LEASE: No modification of this lease shall be binding unless in writing and executed by the parties hereto.

BINDING ON HEIRS: It is further agreed that this lease and all covenants and agreements herein contained shall accrue to and be binding upon the parties hereto, their heirs, successors, administrators, executors and assigns.

IN WITNESS WHEREOF, the Owner and Lessee have executed the lease the day and year above written:

_____ (Owner)

_____ (Lessee)

STATE OF _____,

COUNTY OF _____, to-wit:

BE IT REMEMBERED, that on this _____ day of _____,
19____ before me, the undersigned, a Notary Public in
and for the County and state aforesaid, came _____,
who is personally known to me to be the same person who
executed the within instrument of writing and such persons duly acknowledged the execution of the same.

IN WITNESS WHEREOF, I have hereunto set my hand and
affixed my notarial seal the day and year last shown above
written.

_____ (Notary Public)
My commission expires _____.

Stud Service Agreement

Date _____

TO _____ (owner of bitch)
_____ (address)

I hereby agree to use my stud dog named _____
A.K.C. Registration Number _____, to breed your bitch
dog named _____, A.K.C. Registration Number _____,
for the sum of $____, payable on the ____ day of _____,
19____.

In the event your said bitch dog does not whelp, you
shall have one free service within one year from date of
breeding at your option.

It is understood and agreed that your bitch dog is free
from infectious, contagious, or transmissible disease or
unsoundness.

It is understood by delivering the said bitch to me that
you agree to the above and that you will pay all transportation costs.

If you accept this agreement, sign the original and one
copy. Return the original to me.

_____ (Owner of Stud Dog)
_____ (Address)

Date _____

I accept the above agreement.

_____ (Owner of Bitch)

Co-Owner Agreement for Stud Dog

TO _____ (Name of Co-Owner)

_____ (Address)

I hereby convey and transfer to you one half interest in a _____ (sex) _____ (breed) dog whelped on the _____ (date), A.K.C. Registration Number _____ for the sum of $_____, the receipt whereof is hereby acknowledged. On and after this date we shall be co-owners and I shall make application to the American Kennel Club for the certificate of registration to be issued in the name of _____ and _____ as co-owners.

Expenses and care of the dog shall be divided as follows: (Here set forth the arrangements for all expenses, care and showing of the dog.)

Stud fees shall be divided as follows: (Here set forth agreement as to breeding arrangements and stud fees.)

You agree to sign all necessary applications for the registration of all offspring as required by the American Kennel Club.

The co-ownership of the dog shall continue (until the _____ day of _____, 19_____) (or for the life of the dog).

Upon the termination of the co-ownership of said dog, other than by death of the dog, you shall sign the certificate of registration authorizing the American Kennel Club to issue a certificate of registration to me as the sole owner.

Signed this _____ day of _____, 19_____, in duplicate.

_____ (Owner)

The undersigned accepts the above co-ownership of said dog in accordance with the terms set forth.

Signed this _____ day of _____, 19_____, in duplicate and returned the original to the owner.

_____ (Co-Owner)

Lease Agreement for Bitch Dog

THIS LEASE executed this _____ day of _____, 19____, by and between _____, hereinafter referred to as "Owner," and _____, hereinafter referred to as "Lessee."

WITNESSETH: Owner does hereby lease to Lessee and Lessee does hereby lease from Owner for a period of _____ months, approximately, beginning the _____ day of _____, 19____ and ending the _____ day of _____, 19____, the following bitch dog:

Name _____

Registration No. _____

Breed _____

RENTAL: The Lessee agrees to pay Owner a total sum of $_____ for the use of the above bitch dog for the lease period to be paid upon the execution of this agreement. In addition, the Lessee agrees to pay the Owner a deposit in the sum of $_____ before delivery of said bitch dog, which deposit will be refunded to the Lessee when he returns the dog to the Owner at the termination of this lease period providing the dog is in good condition (approximately the same condition as when accepted by the Lessee at the beginning of the lease period).

Lessee warrants that he (has)(has not) inspected said dog and agrees to accept this dog in his present condition. Lessee shall pay and provide for the transportation of the dog from Owner to the Lessee and for the return of said dog to Owner at _____ at the expiration of the lease. Lessee shall not obligate Owner for any expense of any kind whatsoever in connection with the leased dog unless authorized in writing by the Owner.

CARE OF DOG: The Lessee, at his expense, shall provide feed, service, equipment and other necessary services for the proper care, maintenance, handling and protection of the leased dog, also veterinary services if needed, all according to the rules of good animal husbandry and reasonable standards and methods of the dog-breeding industry. Owner shall have the right at any time, in person, or by authorized agent, to go upon the Lessee's premises to inspect the dog, and to determine if properly cared for and in good health.

The Owner shall assign the registration certificate to the Lessee for the purpose of permitting the Lessee to register the offspring of this dog resulting from breeding her. Upon the termination of this lease the Lessee shall assign the registration certificate to the Owner.

The title and ownership of the leased dog shall be and remain in the name of Owner. Lessee shall not sell, mortgage or encumber in any manner whatsoever this leased dog.

Lessee shall hold Owner harmless for any injury to persons or damages to any property caused by this leased dog. Lessee shall not permit the leased dog to be seized or impounded by anyone because of damages to property of others. Lessee shall pay when due any taxes which may be levied by any city, township, county, state or other taxing body wherein said leased dog may be located during the term of said lease. Lessee shall not assign this lease nor sublease this dog covered hereby.

If the leased dog should at any time become missing, lost, estrayed, seriously injured, sick, or dead, the Lessee shall immediately notify Owner by telephone and subsequently by mail. There shall be no abatement of rental paid due to death of leased dog if the dog dies during the period for which the rental has already been paid.

In the event the bitch does not whelp a litter from the first breeding season, the Lessee may breed her at the next breeding season and return the bitch after the offspring are weaned. If the bitch does not produce offspring within

75 days after the second season breeding, this lease shall terminate and the Lessee shall return the bitch to the Owner as hereinabove provided.

MODIFICATION OF LEASE: No modification of this lease shall be binding unless in writing and executed by the parties hereto.

BINDING ON HEIRS: It is further agreed that this lease and all covenants and agreements herein contained shall accrue to and be binding upon the parties hereto, their heirs, successors, administrators, executors and assigns.

IN WITNESS WHEREOF, the Owner and the Lessee have executed the lease the day and year first above written:

_____ (Owner)

_____ (Lessee)

Co-Owner Agreement for Bitch Dog

To _____ (Name)

_____ (Address)

I hereby convey and transfer to you one-half interest in a _____(sex) _____(breed) dog whelped on the _____(date), A.K.C. Registration Number _____ for the sum of $_____, the receipt whereof is hereby acknowledged. On and after this date we shall be co-owners and I shall make application to the American Kennel Club for the certificate of registration to be issued in the name of _____ and _____, as co-owners.

Expenses and care of the dog shall be divided as follows: (Here set forth the arrangements for all expenses, care and showing of the dog.)

Breeding arrangements shall be as follows: (Here set forth the arrangements for breeding and dividing the offspring.)

You agree to sign all necessary applications for the registration of all offspring as required by the American Kennel Club.

The co-ownership of the dog shall continue (until the ____ day of _____, 19____) (or for the life of the dog).

Upon the termination of the co-ownership of said dog, other than by death of the dog, you shall sign the certificate of registration authorizing the American Kennel Club to issue a certificate of registration to me as the sole owner.

Signed this ____ day of _____, 19____, in duplicate.

_____ (Owner)

The undersigned accepts the above co-ownership of said dog in accordance with the terms set forth.

Signed this ____ day of _____, 19____, in duplicate and returned the original to the owner.

_____ (Co-Owner)

Lease Agreement for Stud Dog

THIS LEASE, executed this ____ day of _____, 19____, by and between _____, hereinafter referred to as "Owner," and _____, hereinafter referred to as "Lessee."

WITNESSETH: Owner does hereby lease to Lessee and Lessee does hereby lease from Owner for a period of ____ months, approximately, beginning the ____ day of _____, 19____, and ending the ____ day of _____, 19____, the following animal:

RENTAL: The Lessee agrees to pay Owner a total sum of $____ for the use of the above dog for the lease period to be paid, _____. In addition, the Lessee agrees to pay the Owner the sum of _____ on or before _____, 19____, which will be refunded to the Lessee when he returns the dog to the Owner at his _____ at the termination of this lease period providing the dog is in good condition (approximately the same condition as when accepted by the Lessee at the beginning of the lease period). Owner also hereby grants the Lessee the option to lease the dog for a second lease period to commence the day following the expiration date of this lease and the second lease period to end on or before the _____ day of _____, 19____, for a total sum of _____ to be paid, $____ the day second lease period starts (_____) and $____ on or before the _____ day of _____, 19____. To exercise the option, the Lessee shall notify the owner in writing at least sixty (60) days prior to the termination of the agreement.

Lessee warrants that he (has) (has not) inspected said dog and agrees to accept this dog in his present condition. Lessee shall pay and provide for the transportation of the dog from Owner to the Lessee and for the return of said dog to Owner at _____ at the expiration of the lease. Lessee shall not obligate Owner for any expense of any kind whatsoever in connection with the leased dog unless authorized in writing by the Owner.

CARE OF DOG: The Lessee, at his expense, shall provide feed, service, equipment and other necessary services for the proper care, maintenance, handling and protection of the leased dog, also Veterinary services if needed, all according to the rules of good animal husbandry and reasonable standards and methods of the dog-breeding industry. Owner shall have the right at any time, in person, or by authorized agent, to go upon the Lessee's premises to inspect the dog, and to determine if properly cared for and in good health.

It is not necessary that Lessee provide death and injury insurance on the leased dog providing he provides good and reasonable care and precautions at all times to prevent injury or death of the dog, and providing if dog becomes sick or injured that Lessee immediately provides for proper veterinary care and attention at Lessee's expense. Owner will not hold Lessee liable for any serious injury or death of the dog while in custody of the Lessee.

The Lessee agrees to provide proper veterinary care

immediately at his expense if the dog becomes sick or injured.

Owner will supply Lessee with such pedigree and registration information as may be needed for registration of future produce of this dog resulting from breeding him to bitches by the Lessee during this lease period. Lessee may stand at Stud the leased dog. Any stud fees collected by the Lessee during the lease period will be the property of Lessee.

Lessee shall hold Owner harmless for any injury to persons or damages to any property caused by this leased dog. Lessee shall not permit the leased dog to be seized or impounded by anyone because of damages to property of others. Lessee shall pay when due any taxes which may be levied by any city, township, county, state or other taxing body wherein said leased dog may be located during the term of said lease. Lessee shall not assign this lease nor sublease this dog covered hereby.

The title and ownership of the leased dog shall be and remain in the name of Owner. Lessee shall not sell, mortgage or encumber in any manner whatsoever this leased dog.

If the leased dog should at any time become missing, lost, estrayed, seriously injured, sick, or dead, the Lessee shall immediately notify Owner by telephone and subsequently by mail. There shall be no abatement of rental paid due to death of leased dog if the dog dies during the period for which the rental has already been paid.

MODIFICATION OF LEASE: No modification of this lease shall be binding unless in writing and executed by the parties hereto.

BINDING ON HEIRS: It is further agreed that this lease and all covenants and agreements herein contained shall accrue to and be binding upon the parties hereto, their heirs, successors, administrators and executors.

IN WITNESS WHEREOF, the Owner and Lessee have executed the lease the day and year above written:

            _____ (Owner)

            _____ (Lessee)

Clauses for Will

Bequest of Dogs

I give, devise and bequest unto _____ all my dogs that I may possess at the time of my death. I hereby express my desire that he care for and dispose of the dogs as I have communicated to him during my life time.

I direct my executor to deliver possession of the dogs to _____ immediately upon my death and to pay all expenses in and about the care of the dogs for _____ _____. (State the period of time.)

All dogs shall be exonerated from liability of the debts of my estate until all other properties both real and personal are first applied.

Bequest

To Take Care of a Pet Dog

I give and bequeath to _____ the sum of $____ and in consideration of my making said bequest to him, he by accepting the same, shall take care at his expense of my dog, _____, as long as she (he) shall live. I direct my executor immediately upon my death to deliver possession of my dog to _____.

INSTALLMENT SALES UNDER UNIFORM COMMERCIAL CODE TO BE USED IN THE FOLLOWING STATES: ALABAMA, ALASKA, ARKANSAS, CALIFORNIA, COLORADO, CONNECTICUT, DISTRICT OF COLUMBIA, FLORIDA, GEORGIA, HAWAII, ILLINOIS, INDIANA, IOWA, KANSAS, KENTUCKY, MAINE,

MARYLAND, MASSACHUSETTS, MICHIGAN, MINNESOTA, MISSOURI, MONTANA, NEBRASKA, NEVADA, NEW HAMP- SHIRE, NEW JERSEY, NEW MEXICO, NEW YORK, NORTH CAROLINA, NORTH DAKOTA, OHIO, OKLAHOMA, OREGON, PENNSYLVANIA, RHODE ISLAND, TENNESSEE, TEXAS, UTAH, VIRGIN ISLANDS, VIRGINIA, WASHINGTON, WEST VIRGINIA, WISCONSIN, AND WYOMING.

Security Agreement

_____ (Date)

(Name) _____ (No. and Street) _____ (City or Town) _____ (County) _____ (State) _____ (here- inafter called Buyer-Debtor), for valuable consideration, receipt whereof is hereby acknowledged, does hereby purchase from, grants to (Name) _____ (No. and Street) _____ (City or Town) _____ (County)_____ (State) _____ (hereinafter called Seller-Secured Party) a security interest and agrees to pay for the described dog(s) being hereinafter called Collateral for a total price and upon and subject to the terms stated below.

DESCRIPTION OF DOGS:

_____(Sex), _____(Breed) dog whelped _____(Date) AKC Reg. No. _____

_____(Sex), _____(Breed) dog whelped _____(Date) AKC Reg. No. _____

TERMS AND PAYMENT:
1. Cash Price $_____
2. Down Payment $_____
3. Unpaid Balance $_____
4. Principal Balance Owing $_____
5. Finance Charges $_____
6. Time Balance—Amt. of Note $_____

Time balance payable in _____ consecutive monthly payments of $_____. (State the number of payments and amounts of other than monthly payments.) First payment due _____ day of _____, 19____.

The conditions of this Security Agreement are such that Buyer has executed and delivered to Seller his certain promissory note of even date herewith and hereinafter referred to as the "Note" in the principal amount equal to the time balance shown above payable as set forth above.

If the obligation hereby secured, or any part thereof, is not paid at the maturity hereof, whether such maturity be caused by lapse of time or by acceleration, such entire obligation, or the part thereof which has matured, as the case may be, shall thereafter draw straight interest at the rate of _____% per annum until paid. Time is of the essence.

In the event there is a default in the payment or conditions of this agreement, the Seller or Secured Party shall have the right to take possession of the said Collateral without notice or at the option of Seller or Secured Party to take such action as is available under the law.

The Collateral will be kept at _____ (Address where dogs are to be kept) except the Buyer shall have the right to transport the said Collateral in the usual course of business of owning, showing, training, exhibiting and hunting dogs. However, the Buyer will notify Seller of any permanent change in location of the Collateral and will not remove the Collateral from the State of _____ without first giving the Seller ten (10) days written notice by registered mail of his intent to change the location and such notice will state the new address in the same detail as above.

Seller warrants that he has good title to said dog(s) and that it is free of all liens and encumbrances.

The Seller will execute all necessary registration certificates and will comply with all requirements of the American Kennel Club relating to the transfer of ownership of the said dog(s) to the Buyer.

_____(Seller-Secured Party)   _____(Buyer-Debtor)

NOTE: The Security Agreement need not be filed. The Financing Statement is filed in the County where the Debtor resides and where the dogs are to be permanently located if at a different location than the residence of the Buyer. In some states there is a central filing. Each State Uniform Commercial Code provides for filing officers. Consult the Code of the State where the dogs are to be located.

Index

143